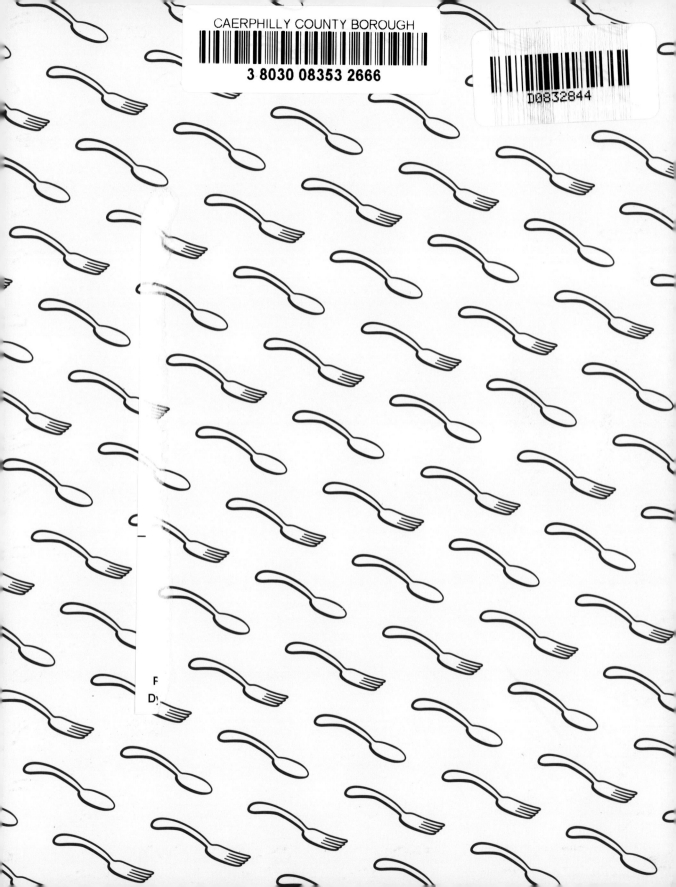

MADE IN THE USA

Florence Cornish

MADE IN THE USA

CLASSIC AND CONTEMPORARY AMERICAN RECIPES FROM COAST TO COAST

PHOTOGRAPHY BY TARA FISHER

Kyle Books

'Food is our common ground,
a universal experience'
James Beard

For my family.
And for all the hungry women.

First published in Great Britain in 2016 by
Kyle Books
an imprint of Kyle Cathie Limited
192-198 Vauxhall Bridge Road
London SW1V 1DX
general.enquiries@kylebooks.com
www.kylebooks.co.uk

10 9 8 7 6 5 4 3 2 1

ISBN: 978 0 85783 354 9

A CIP catalogue record for this title is available from the
British Library

Florence Cornish is hereby identified as the author of this
work in accordance with Section 77 of the Copyright, Designs
and Patents Act 1988.

Text © Florence Cornish 2016
Photographs © Tara Fisher 2016
Design © Kyle Books 2016

Editor: Vicky Orchard
Design and illustrations: Sarah Greeno
sarahgreeno.com limitededitiondesign.co.uk
Photography: Tara Fisher
Food styling: Joss Herd
Props styling: Tabitha Hawkins
Production: Nic Jones and Gemma John

Colour reproduction by F1 colour, London
Printed and bound in China by 1010 International Printing Ltd.

CONTENTS

/ **Introduction**
Page 6

1/ **Breakfasts & Brunches**
Page 14

2/ **Burgers, Barbecue & Slow Cooking**
Page 40

3/ **Home Comforts & Modern Classics**
Page 66

4/ **Cajun, Creole & Southern Delicacies**
Page 88

5/ **Mexican Delights**
Page 112

6/ **Baking & Sweet Treats**
Page 134

7/ **Drinks & Tipples**
Page 158

/ **Index**
Page 174

INTRODUCTION

It's 30 degrees, around 8pm on a Friday night, and I'm on the hunt for fried chicken. Not just any fried chicken. I'm in Memphis, Tennessee, so naturally, I'm after Gus's World Famous Fried Chicken. In my guide book, a lone dollar sign signalling cheap eats and a review proclaiming something along the lines of 'If you don't go here to eat, you may as well have not even come to Tennessee because this chicken will change your life' means that there is no way I'm leaving on the Greyhound tomorrow without eating some. So, after creepily trotting behind two women who mentioned 'chicken' and 'die happy', I find it. Chequered table cloths, plastic plates, cookies wrapped in clingfilm at the cash register being sold for a dollar – Toto, I'm not in Kansas or Crystal Palace anymore – I'm in nirvana. I'm in the deepest of the Deep South and I never want to leave.

I have been in love with all things American for as long as I can remember. There is not a moment in my life when I was not watching American TV, eating American food, travelling the States, listening to American bands – it shaped me more than just during my formative years. I'm still as obsessed with the entire culture, history, politics, cuisine and language of this nation. When I was three, my family and I moved to Sarasota, Florida. From Singapore, to Thailand, to Indonesia and Belgium, we bounced around a lot, so the small town of Sarasota, Florida, was another stop on our itinerant youth. Sarasota is the home of the Nick Bollettieri Tennis Academy, which churns out the town's second biggest export, after Tropicana Orange Juice. It was the juice that brought us here, as my dad worked for the company. My mum likes to remind us how on hot, dry days you couldn't go anywhere without being smothered by the marmalade-y, burnt orange cloud hovering over the sleepy town. Both nauseating and nostalgic – kind of like thinking about an ex-boyfriend or remembering teen haircuts. When we hopped off the plane in the steamy, stormy, Sunshine State, that – was – it. I had found a place where Barney the Dinosaur played on repeat (teaching me everything I

know today), where the Magic Kingdom was only an hour away and where slices of pie were the size of a young child. The sun bleached my light-brown hair and our sponge-like brains and chameleon accents became full-on U. S. of A. 'Mummy' was now 'Momma', 'trainers' now 'sneakers' and me, 'Miss America' – a title given me by my dentist, which I've decided to have etched on my gravestone.

America became home and the food became my go-to cuisine. Everything we ate had a story, a reason for existing that went so much deeper than the need to eat. Pateli's Pizza, our favourite local haunt, was started by an Indian family who, after realising a gap in the market, stuck an 'i' on the end of their name and proceeded to make some of the best pizza around. If that's not the American Dream, I don't know what is. It was the same with the Amish cafeteria my mum loved to go to, for their ENORMOUS pies. I think the rule is, if the whipped cream isn't at least triple the height of the pie, you're not doing it right. Clouds of white, pillowy cream, sweet, salted, roasted peanuts and the shortest pastry – no wonder by the time we zipped back to Europe my cheeks were more hamster-like than ever.

And this is what I was so drawn in by and what I love so much about American food.

Every single dish has a story behind it, a reason for being that runs deeper than any other cuisine I can think of.

One of the greatest things about American food is the roots that ground it in the past and connect it to the present. I am an out-and-proud, full-blown history nerd – studying it through school and university, and now I genuinely dread the idea of a

commute longer than two minutes without my Stuff You Missed in History Class podcast. Almost every single American dish, right down to the exact variety of potato used or grape harvested, isn't just there by chance. If you're eating a po' boy sandwich, you're

probably paying $5 for something named after the New Orleans dock workers – people who used to ask for scraps at the back doors of restaurant kitchens after a shift, too broke to go inside and order something. If you're making a lobster roll, you are cooking the exact ingredient that was so plentiful in the early days of the Maine settlement, that it was used as bait to catch cod – I almost cried with despair when I discovered this. Imagine all those lobsters. For COD?!

This food is not just traditional, or old-fashioned, or typical. It is a living connection to the past. More so than art, or music, or architecture – everybody eats.

Like James Beard said 'Food is our common ground, a universal experience'. He also said that 'Too few people understand a really good sandwich', so, clearly, he was a genius. There is nothing else that someone from the tiniest village in Thailand to a businessman in Austin, Texas, has in common more so than food. Everybody enjoys food in one way or another, and it is this that, I think, showcases what people's lives were really like, and are really like. You can tell a lot about someone from the company they keep. You can tell even more from what they eat for lunch with that company.

So who am I, right? Like, who is this chick? I'm not American, I've got no family there and, apart from always being on the look-out for a guy with a green card, I'm not about to move there right this second. Although if anyone knows of a job opening…

Well, all I can say is that if the US wants to get rid of me, they better call security because I'm going to be like the crazy ex-girlfriend at the wedding. Sticking. A - Round. I lived in the States as a kid and went back to work at Walt Disney World in Florida when I was twenty. I have travelled more parts of the US than I can honestly remember and have spent an embarrassingly large amount of time reading about, listening to and generally studying up on all things American. So I like to think I'm quite clued up. Let's say I wouldn't be able to take on a tenured teaching post in US history, but I would pick it as my special subject for *Mastermind*. Somewhere in between.

I am so truly an Americophile that there is nothing to me that would be dreamier than packing up, moving to a cabin somewhere deep in the Smoky Mountains, cooking, reading and writing about the US for the rest of my days.

My history teacher in school was a hell of a woman. She was intelligent (as you would hope), well travelled, encouraging, keen for debate – one of those people you are always just a little bit afraid of but equally want to impress. Paula Hailstone wasn't fluffy around the edges. She wasn't one to say 'You tried your best and that's enough'. She was one to say 'Try harder, study more, read more, understand deeper'. It wasn't enough to scratch the surface of history; with her, you had to know why something happened, when, why did it matter, who was affected, who else could be affected – in short, everything to do with the subject. 'Depth of knowledge' was the phrase pounded into us and I've remembered it all this time for a reason. It's not enough to just think that snickerdoodles are a funny name for a cookie, or that a po' boy is just a sandwich – you have to understand and respect the way these foods came to be and the people that brought them into existence. There would have been a German family who left everything behind to sail the week-long journey to the US, settled in New England and baked foods that reminded them of home, while trying to readjust to a completely new life. Those Schneckennudel, or cinnamon-raisin buns, became snickerdoodles and in turn, established themselves as part of a totally new baking culture, unlike any other in the world. You have to understand and respect these dishes as a way of respecting the people who created them. They were real people, who lived real, difficult lives, and the food we have should be shown the admiration they deserve.

I have found so much joy in cooking these recipes, researching their backgrounds,

learning about their creators, and sharing them with my friends and family.

I suppose that's what I'm drawn to most about American food – the fact that it is totally about sharing.

Food is spread out on a table, with dishes passed back and forth, everyone piling their plates high and arguments erupting over who gets the last yam. Ahhh, family. There is no separation between what's mine and what's yours. It's ours and it's collective. American food is exactly that – belonging to everyone and adored by all.

THE BUILDING BLOCKS OF THE AMERICAN TABLE

This list is my personal opinion of what constitutes the very core of what it is to eat the food of the USA – bearing in mind it is a country more diverse than anywhere else in the world with a vast food culture. There will no doubt be those who disagree with this list, but I feel it is a great way to gain a little insight into what the soul and spirit of American food is, regardless of whether it has an Hispanic, Native American, Jewish or English origin.

MEAT

Trying to think of a barbecue without beef, pork and chicken is impossible. Trying to think of Thanksgiving without turkey? Or Christmas without ham? What is this unwinnable challenge?!

America and meat are almost synonymous. Without cattle, pigs and chickens, you would be hard-pressed to chart a true path of American cuisine. In a way similar to Australia, the vast empty plains of the USA were wide open, literally, for farmers to graze large herds of animals on, slaughtering them and making an impressive business in the meantime. It also meant that meat was a lot cheaper in the New World than back in Europe, where smaller lands meant smaller yields and higher prices.

So meat is typically a much more egalitarian ingredient than in other parts of the world, where it was pricey and prized, in equal measure. The fact that you could have bacon for breakfast, roast chicken for lunch and meatloaf for dinner shows how meat was for the masses, not just the elite.

It varies, like anything, hugely in quality, but the very universality of it gives an insight into something very interesting about the American table – no food is out of bounds, no food is exclusive, no food is too good for you. So bring on the bacon.

BUTTERMILK

Buttermilk is so essential to American cooking, and baking in particular, that you simply CANNOT bake authentically without it. Having tried to substitute it with everything from cream to yogurt to just regular milk, it's that buttery by-product you need to make it all taste right. And there's a science to it. Buttermilk is naturally acidic, because it ferments while the cream that will be churned into butter separates and floats to the top of whatever vessel you are holding the milk in. (Although these days it tends to be cultured en masse and boxed up for sale because, well, we're not living on the prairies anymore.) This means that when it's mixed with bicarbonate of soda (an alkali) it fizzes and foams, and produces CO_2 that makes your baked goods rise up. Your cakes will end up being lighter than air and fluffier than you could ever imagine. It makes for a tender crumb in biscuits and a dangerously delicious crispy fried chicken coating.

It's hard to say why buttermilk is still so commonly used in the States, but I would put it down to the fact that it hasn't been so long since those frontier-families were pushing West and making do with traditional cooking techniques. If you had to make your own butter by leaving it to ferment, you would probably shove buttermilk into everything too. So the fact that this tradition is still quite close to modern cooking techniques might help to explain the prevalence of this delectable dairy product in recipes, where in other parts of the world we have let it fall by the wayside.

CHILLI

To ignore the Latino, and in particular, Mexican influence on US culinary history, would be to ignore one of the largest and most important parts of it. Spanish colonies played a key role in shaping American history, holding control over what we know today as Florida, California, New Mexico and Texas, among others. And their influence in these areas is immense. To look at houses in Southern Spain is almost like looking straight into Pasadena, California. And the flavour profiles are just as steadfast.

Chillies find themselves in all sorts of aspects of US food – from hot sauces, to pizza toppings, to tacos, salsa and beyond. They have spread much further than just Mexican cuisine, diversifying along their route. The chilli spice of Creole cooking, for instance, is musky and preserved, echoing a history based around shipping foods down the Mississippi river, and so needing them to last. The heat of New Mexican is fresh and fiery, with no hint of letting up for those not used to the punch. Whereas in California, you have the appropriately named 'Anaheim' chilli that scores low on the Scoville scale but high on flavour, for the less red-blooded among us.

To imagine American food without chillies would be to imagine it without that undertone of piquancy that carries each dish through. You might not realise it, but like the best friend in a romcom, it was there all along.

SYRUP

Like corn or yams, maple syrup was harvested and enjoyed by Native Americans long before European settlers even thought about pouring it over pancakes. It was a natural sweetener and seasoning, as well as being harvested to provide much-needed energy and calories to get through harsh winters.

Nowadays, maple syrup is breakfast. Pancakes, waffles, bacon, oatmeal, hams – they all get a gloss of the golden stuff. It was (as with a lot of native foods) the European settlers who latched on to maple, tapping and turning it into an industry for export and profit. Maple syrup then spread across the entire United States – far beyond its original North-Eastern parameters – becoming fully entrenched in the American storecupboard. But maple syrup also became a symbol of abolitionism, when anti-slavery campaigners boycotted the sugar cane and molasses of the South to instead wave the maple flag of freedom. Maple was natural, it was produced with paid labour and was available for all.

There are a lot of people who only see the unhealthy side of American food and believe me, there is one. But there is one in all cuisines, and to focus on it exclusively would be to ignore the balance and delicate flavour of these ingredients. Maple syrup is rich, earthy, warming and nutty, with so much more to offer than just saccharine sweetness. The thought of having a short stack of pancakes without that glorious amber nectar?! Please, don't scare me.

SMOKE

Smoke is one of the oldest methods of preserving foods, especially meats, and was used by the Native Americans way before Europeans even thought there was a New World. Because there is such an abundance of great smoking wood trees in the States, such as cherry, hickory, apple and maple, smoking soon became an art. You would be hard-pressed to travel through the States today and not come across some form of smoked meat – be it brisket, ribs, chicken...

Smoking in the Southern States tends to be hot smoking, but at a fairly low temperature (usually 90–120°C) for an untold amount of hours. This means you get the charred, earthy flavour as well as slow cooking the meat itself, hence why tougher cuts like brisket, ribs and pork shoulder are most often found in barbecue food. This type of smoking needs a purpose-built smoker, outside where the excess can escape easily and you can leave it running for as long as you need. So it's a little tricky to try at home. However, you can easily build your own stove-top smoker, which will do a similar process but much faster – usually in about 30 minutes. Or try liquid smoke, which is quite literally condensed barbecue smoke. It's made in a very similar way to how spirits are distilled, where you heat a liquid to steam (or smoke) and then cool it rapidly, turning it back into a liquid. It's super-intense in flavour and if you add a few drops to your dish, you can have all the effect of the grill and none of the mess.

FISH

Because America is so vast and so many of the States are land-locked, it can be easy to forget the coasts. East- and West-coast America have some of the best fish in the world. You couldn't go to Maine and not have lobster, and it doesn't bear thinking about to go to California and not have fish tacos. Fish is such a staple protein and a fantastic example of how sometimes a cuisine is not best shaped by techniques, processes and refinement, but by the quality of the natural ingredients found on its shores.

Right down to the Bayou, fish and seafood have often been so popular because of their cheaper price. By their nature, wild fish don't require farming or feeding and so can be plucked right out of the ocean and sold for whatever they'll fetch. Or at least this was how it used to be. As towns and cities grew and people needed to be fed, these once-cheap fish were priced higher and higher and so became much more of a luxury.

But fish is still a keystone of American cuisine, and not to think of it in this way would be a crying shame. After all, this is the land of surf 'n' turf, clam bakes and lobster broils. America would not have flourished without the incredible produce found in its lakes, rivers and oceans, and so is most definitely a building block of the archetypal American table.

CORN

For anyone who has seen the Disney version
of Pocahontas, you will remember that classic
scene where the princess offers a corn on the
cob to John Smith when he bluntly tells her
that him and his ship-sailing buddies are
looking for gold. That one snippet of
historical cartoonism shows just how
fundamental corn is in the American diet,
both Native and New.

Corn, or maize, is the staple grain of the
USA, growing naturally and in abundance.
The US is number one in the world for corn
production, with Iowa dominating the state-
by-state production figures. And somewhat
incredibly, 95 per cent of all corn-producing
farmlands are still family owned! Pretty
amazing, if you ask me.

Corn finds its way into every part of the
American diet, through breakfast muffins,
to cornbread and grits, to lemon chess pie
and hushpuppies – there is no way you can go
to the States and not eat corn. Like pumpkin,
corn is often offered up at Thanksgiving as
a kind of vegetable truce or symbol of peace
at the shared dinner table between Native
Americans and new settlers. I don't know
how effective an image or offering that is,
considering the very difficult history that
was to follow, but what I do love about corn
and why I feel it's so intrinsic to the
American diet is that shared experience
of it. America may run on Dunkin' but it
lives on maize.

RICE

Rice may not come to your mind when you
think of the typical American table, but
without it you are blindsiding a huge part
of the Deep South that lived off rice, both
as an income and foodstuff, for centuries.

The grain came over to the USA in the
seventeenth century along with African
slaves. The boggy, hot lands of Georgia and
South Carolina had the ideal conditions for
growing it and plantation owners saw a gap
in the market that few others were competing
for. The slaves, who had grown rice back on
their native continent, brought with them
expert techniques in planting, harvesting and
storing rice, making significant profits for
their owners. The variety of grain grown most
commonly during this time was 'Carolina Gold'
which says more than a little about the value
of that white grain.

Rice production died out with the end
of slavery, but its importance to American
cooking did not. Because rice could be sold
in large quantities as cheap filler, it
flourished in the states where it was grown,
particularly in peasant foods like jambalaya
and gumbo. Poorer people embraced the grain
as a way to stretch more expensive
ingredients, and in turn, made it totally
intertwined with the culture and cuisine
of their region – notably Creole cooking.
You can't eat Creole food without rice and
you can't appreciate its importance without
knowing where it came from and why.

BREAK

☞ AN

BRUN

FASTS

ND ☞

CHES

Is there any meal in the world more
wonderful than breakfast? Answer: no.
For so many, many questions,
the answer is simply 'breakfast'.

'I'm dying from this hangover, nothing in life has hurt this much, I can't move… How can I make it through this Thursday?'

Breakfast.

'I have to get to work at 4am tomorrow because someone dropped out and they need cover. What could possibly make this worth my time?'

Breakfast.

'It's a Friday night, I have a date with Netflix and Ben & Jerry's, but I feel like I'm missing something… What is it?'

Breakfast. (Granted with this one, you could substitute Friday for any day of the week.)

That meal, first thing in the morning or just after two o'clock in the afternoon if you're doing your Sunday right, is just glorious. It can be so special if you take a little time to give it the attention it deserves. Now, I am the first one to reach for the cereal bowl at five to eight in the morning when I'm falling out the door to make it to work on time, but come on people! Let's give brekkie a little love for once. After all, it treats us so well.

I don't know about you, but a nice breakfast always gets me in such a good mood for the day. Because good breakfast, in whatever

Freudian-psycho-Doctor-Phil way it figures, transports me back to holidays. If it's pancakes and waffles, I'm right back at Disney World, aged five or twenty-three, eating Mickey Mouse-shaped waffles drowning in maple syrup, with piles of golden, glistening bacon. Or if it's French toast, it's the weekend, and I have a day off where I can make what is essentially a dessert, for my most important meal of the day. Or if it's eggs Benedict, then that's Christmas, kid! It whips you right back to that happy place, for at least as long as your plate's full.

Now, I would never go so far, or be as annoyingly chipper, as to call myself a morning person, so I've deliberately designed these recipes to be as morning friendly as possible. That is not to say get up at the crack of dawn to start shredding potatoes for latkes or heating up the waffle iron. None of the recipes you'll find in this chapter are going to make you hide under the covers until it's an acceptable time to order pizza (10.45am, in my experience). They are here to help you celebrate those pre-noon hours, where pyjamas are the dress code and messy hair mandatory. Plus, BONUS, all these recipes can be served very easily on a tray. In bed. Made by someone else. With fresh coffee. Just a tip…

BAGELS WITH HOME-CURED LOX AND SCHMEAR

FOR THE BAGELS

450–600g salmon fillet,
  skinned and pin-boned
1 tablespoon whole black
  peppercorns, lightly crushed
200g sea salt flakes
130g granulated sugar
a large bunch of fresh dill,
  roughly chopped
a large bunch of fresh flat-leaf
  parsley, roughly chopped
2 tablespoons vodka
5 good-quality bagels
250g full-fat cream cheese
60g capers
1 lemon, to serve
freshly ground black pepper,
  to taste

SERVES 5

Bagels lavishly spread with cream cheese, strewn with strips of tangerine salmon and topped off with a sprinkling of capers and black pepper are about as New Yoik as you can get. They are the Jewish bread and butter of the deli world – the perfect balance of flavours, textures and memories.

'Lox' is the original name for what would be the belly off-cuts of the salmon fillet, cured solely in salt to render them quite firm and seriously saline.

❶ Remove the brown layer of flesh on the salmon using a sharp knife then cut it in half through the width of the fillet.

❷ On a work surface, lay down three layers of clingfilm large enough to wrap around the salmon easily. In a bowl, mix together the peppercorns, salt, sugar, dill, parsley and vodka. Spread one-third of the mixture on the clingfilm and place half the salmon on top.

❸ Cover the salmon with another third of the salt mixture and place the other half of the fish on top of that. Finish with a final layer of curing salt and then wrap really tightly in clingfilm. Pop the parcel onto a shallow baking tray (or a container with a lip to avoid any juices leaking) and place another tray on top, weighing the top tray down with cans or anything heavy that will squish down the salmon. Transfer to the fridge to cure overnight.

❹ The next morning, flip the fish over, weight it down again and refrigerate for another day. When the salmon is sufficiently cured, scrape off the excess salt and sugar mixture, and wipe the flesh with damp kitchen paper. Use your sharpest knife to slice the salmon, cutting super-thin strips across the width of the fillet at a 45-degree angle.

❺ Slice the bagels in half, place them cut-side up on a baking tray and toast lightly under the grill before spreading each half liberally with the cream cheese.

❻ Drain the capers and rinse them under cold running water to remove most of the briny flavour. Cut the lemon into wedges, picking out any seeds, and set aside.

❼ Pile the bagels high with salmon and finish with a few capers, a squeeze of lemon juice and some black pepper.

OLD-FASHIONED WAFFLES WITH MAPLE BACON

FOR THE WAFFLES

310g plain flour

2 tablespoons caster sugar

½ teaspoon salt

1 tablespoon baking powder

290ml milk

1 teaspoon vanilla extract

70ml vegetable oil, plus extra
   for greasing

2 eggs, lightly beaten

FOR THE MAPLE BACON
----

16 rashers unsmoked streaky
   bacon

4 tablespoons maple syrup,
   plus extra for serving

SERVES 4

I first came across maple bacon when I was working in Florida. I came home after a shift to find my housemate cooking. The sweet, nutty, salty aroma that floated from the stove was enough to stop me dead in my tracks and ask where exactly she had bought it and how much it cost. Sadly, it's tricky to get pre-mapled bacon outside the US (what is the world coming to?!), so here is a recipe for making your own.

----

❶ Preheat the oven to 200°C/gas mark 6 and preheat a greased waffle iron to a medium heat. If you like your waffles really crispy, then go for a higher heat, but medium should leave you a little crust with a pillowy inside.

❷ To make the waffles, put the flour, sugar, salt and baking powder in a freestanding mixer and mix together well.

❸ Whisk the milk, vanilla, oil and eggs together in a jug. Gradually add the liquid ingredients to the dry ones, with the mixer motor running. You should end up with a smooth, fairly thick batter.

❹ Spread a ladleful of batter onto the waffle iron, taking care not to overfill it. Close the lid and cook for 6 minutes until golden and crisp. Keep the waffles warm while you cook their relatives.

❺ For the maple bacon, place the bacon on a wire rack over a roasting tin and cook for 10–12 minutes in the oven until really crispy. Check the bacon to see if it's crispy enough (don't settle for flabby rashers, people), brush all over with the maple syrup and pop back in the oven for 5 minutes.

❻ Serve the waffles piled high with bacon and doused in more maple syrup.

RED VELVET PANCAKES WITH CREAM CHEESE DRIZZLE

FOR THE PANCAKES

290g plain flour

30g cocoa powder

50g caster sugar

2 tablespoons baking powder

1 teaspoon bicarbonate of soda

2 eggs, lightly beaten

420ml milk

1 tablespoon red food colouring gel or paste (it must be gel or paste, not liquid, or it will mess up the proportions, making the colour dull and the batter too loose)

1 teaspoon vegetable oil

FOR THE CREAM CHEESE DRIZZLE

45g icing sugar

200g full-fat cream cheese

1 teaspoon milk

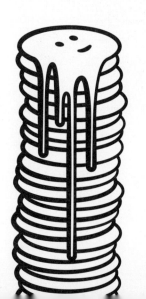

SERVES 6 (MAKES 8-12 PANCAKES)

In *The Taste of America*, Colman Andrews says red velvet cake 'at its best… is moist and dense but not overly sugary, with a subtle glow of chocolate', and my God is he right.

I will not have a bad word said against red velvet. It. Is. My. Favourite. I can only say this; I ADORE IT. There is no other flavour that makes people go 'Oh wow!', in the same way as when someone takes a piece of red velvet. I wanted to get that same reaction from breakfast; this is for birthdays and celebrations, or maybe just every other Wednesday.

❶ To make the pancakes, put the flour, cocoa powder, sugar, baking powder and bicarbonate of soda into the bowl of a freestanding mixer. Mix thoroughly, but be gentle.

❷ Mix the eggs, milk and food colouring in a jug, and gradually add to the dry ingredients, occasionally scraping down the sides with a spatula to ensure a smooth batter.

❸ Heat the oil in a large frying pan and then wipe out as much of it as possible with kitchen paper. Ladle small amounts of the batter into the pan and smooth with the back of the ladle to form little circles, about 7cm across. Cook until you see bubbles in the middle of the pancakes and the edges turning from glossy blood red to a slightly matte tone.

❹ Once at this stage, carefully flip and continue to cook for 1 minute on the other side. Remove from the pan and keep warm while you cook the remaining pancakes.

❺ Then, make the drizzle. In a bowl, sift the icing sugar and pop the cream cheese and milk on top. Using a spatula, beat together and spoon into a piping bag.

❻ Once you are ready to serve, pile the pancakes as high as you like and drizzle with the cream cheese.

NEVER-FAIL PANCAKES WITH BANANAS FOSTER

FOR THE PANCAKES

310g plain flour

50g caster sugar

2 tablespoons baking powder

1 teaspoon bicarbonate of soda

1 teaspoon salt

2 eggs, lightly beaten

420ml buttermilk

50ml milk

1 teaspoon vegetable oil

FOR THE BANANAS FOSTER

110g salted butter

80g soft dark brown sugar

4 ripe bananas, cut into 4cm
   chunks on the diagonal

60ml spiced rum

pinch of sea salt

SERVES 6 (MAKES 8-12 PANCAKES)

My mum makes AMAZING pancakes. I don't know how she does it. They are light, fluffy, golden and crisp all at once. However! This recipe is a pretty good alternative. The buttermilk is essential because the acid in it reacts with the baking powder and bicarb to get the cakes puffy rather than sad and soggy.

Bananas Foster are truly a dessert. But I feel no guilt suggesting them for breakfast because, well… banana's a fruit. The dish was eponymously named after Richard Foster, a friend of an Owen Brennan who owned the restaurant that created the dish in 1951. This dessert SCREAMS New Orleans, to me. Rum, heady spice and dark sugar – you can pretty much taste NOLA when you take a bite.

----

❶ To make the pancakes, put the flour, sugar, baking powder, bicarbonate of soda and salt in the bowl of a freestanding mixer and stir together thoroughly.

❷ Whisk the eggs, buttermilk and milk in a jug. Gradually add to the flour mixture, scraping through occasionally with a spatula to make sure there aren't any sneaky lumps.

❸ Heat the oil in a large frying pan and then wipe out as much as possible with kitchen paper. Ladle small amounts of the batter into the pan and smooth with the back of the ladle to form little circles, about 7cm across. Cook until you see bubbles appearing in the middle of the pancakes and then flip, with care. Continue to cook until golden brown on that side. Remove from the pan and keep warm while you cook the remaining pancakes.

❹ For the bananas, melt the butter in a high-sided frying pan and add the sugar. Caramelise slightly and then add the bananas, spreading evenly. Cook for a minute or so, until softened on the outside, then pour over the rum, lighting with a match to flambé off the excess alcohol. Finally, sprinkle with the sea salt.

❺ Pile the pancakes high with bananas foster and feel smug at the fact that you got two shots in before lunch.

BLUEBERRY AND CINNAMON PANCAKES

FOR THE PANCAKES

310g plain flour

50g caster sugar

2 tablespoons baking powder

1 teaspoon bicarbonate of soda

½ teaspoon ground cinnamon

zest of 1 lemon

1 teaspoon salt

2 eggs, lightly beaten

420ml buttermilk

50ml milk

1 teaspoon vegetable oil

150g blueberries

maple syrup, to serve

SERVES 6 (MAKES 8-12 PANCAKES)

One thing that is fabulous about pancakes — and the Never-fail pancakes (page 23) in particular — is that they are so adaptable. You can mix and match, pick and mix whatever flavours, fruits, berries and nuts you want to go in there. The breakfast plate is your oyster.

----

❶ Make the batter as for the Never-fail pancakes (page 23) including the ground cinnamon and lemon zest.

❷ Heat the oil in a large frying pan and then wipe out as much as possible with kitchen paper.

❸ Ladle small amounts of the batter into the pan and smooth each one into a circle shape, about 7cm across, with the base of the ladle. Pop 3-4 blueberries on top of each pancake. Cook until you see bubbles appearing in the middle of the pancakes and then flip, with care. Continue to cook until golden brown on that side. Remove from the pan and keep warm.

❹ Serve with gallons of maple syrup and fresh black coffee. A true American classic.

LATKES WITH CHILLI TOMATO RELISH AND FRIED EGGS

FOR THE CHILLI TOMATO RELISH

2 tablespoons olive oil
1 medium white onion, finely
  diced
1 garlic clove, crushed
1 teaspoon dried oregano
½ teaspoon dried chilli flakes
½ teaspoon smoked sweet paprika
400g can chopped tomatoes
1 tablespoon tomato purée
1 tablespoon chilli jam
1 teaspoon maple syrup

FOR THE LATKES

450g floury potatoes, peeled
  and coarsely grated
salt
1 egg, lightly beaten
white pepper, to taste
good grating of whole nutmeg
50ml vegetable oil, for frying
4 eggs
soured cream, to serve
  (optional)

SERVES 4 (MAKES 8 LARGE LATKES)

Latkes are essentially a kind of rough rösti, fried in lots of oil and flavoured with onion and egg. Because of their oily cooking method, latkes are traditionally eaten at Hanukkah, but just like sugar cookies at Christmas or candy by the truckload at Halloween, I think it is a real shame that it is socially snubbed to eat this kind of food all year round. So this recipe is a little twist for a fabulous way to get your eggs in the morning.

❶ To make the chilli tomato relish, heat the oil in a small saucepan. Sweat the onion, covered with some dampened baking parchment, over a low heat for about 15 minutes until softened. Transfer half the onion to a separate bowl.

❷ Add the garlic to the remaining onion and cook for about 1 minute until aromatic. Add the oregano, chilli flakes and paprika, and cook for a further minute. Tip in the tomatoes, tomato purée, chilli jam and maple syrup, bring to the boil and reduce to a simmer for about 20 minutes.

❸ Meanwhile, start on the latkes. Put the grated potatoes in a colander and sprinkle generously with salt. Leave to drain for about 10 minutes.

❹ Place large handfuls of potato in a clean tea towel and squeeze out all the moisture. Then plop into a large mixing bowl. Add the beaten egg along with the reserved sweated onion, some salt, white pepper and nutmeg to taste. Heat the vegetable oil in a shallow frying pan and spoon a heaped dessertspoon of mixture into the pan. Flatten the top with the back of the spoon until the latke is about 7cm in diameter.

❺ Fry for 1 minute until golden on one side, then flip and cook on the other side for a further minute. Once done, drain on kitchen paper and sprinkle with a little salt. Repeat with the remaining mixture.

❻ Fry the eggs in a little of the vegetable oil to your preferred doneness. (I'm a sunny-side-up kinda girl, every time.) Serve the latkes with a large dollop of chilli tomato relish, the eggs and soured cream, if you like.

REDNECK
EGGS BENEDICT

----

1 quantity of Quick and easy
  cornbread (page 33)
1 quantity of Maple bacon
  (page 20)

FOR THE HOLLANDAISE
----

3 egg yolks
2 tablespoons white wine
  vinegar
salt, to taste
white pepper, to taste
pinch of cayenne pepper
150g salted butter, melted
4 eggs
2 spring onions, finely sliced
  on the diagonal

SERVES 2

Eggs Benedict is the Godfather of breakfast dining. Regal, old
school, the epitome of class. But then I thought, Hey! Why not
do what I do best and make it delicious *and* trashy all at the
same time?! Take away the English muffin and usher in golden,
moist cornbread. Thinly sliced honey-glazed ham? Mmm, how
about bacon, cured in maple syrup? And a flourish of freshly
chopped parsley on top is now replaced with sharp, tangy
spring onions.

----

❶ Make the cornbread and maple bacon. Set aside while you make
   the eggs and hollandaise.

❷ Make the hollandaise by placing the egg yolks in a heatproof
   bowl set over a pan of just-simmering water. Add 1 tablespoon
   of the white wine vinegar, a pinch of salt, white pepper and
   cayenne, and mix.

❸ Whisking continuously with a balloon whisk, slowly pour in
   the melted butter, watching it thicken. If it becomes too
   stiff, let it down with a splash of tepid water. Once made,
   closely cover right onto the surface of the hollandaise with
   a piece of clingfilm and keep warm.

❹ To poach the eggs, heat a large saucepan of water with the
   remaining 1 tablespoon of white wine vinegar. Crack the
   eggs, one at a time, into a mug. Once the water is at a
   poach (where small bubbles occasionally break the surface),
   stir using a slotted spoon to create a whirlpool and gently
   pour in the egg. Let the egg find itself (like a gap-year
   kid) and cook for 1–2 minutes, for a runny yolk.

❺ Serve wedges of cornbread, topped with bacon rashers, two
   eggs per person, plus a generous spoonful of hollandaise and
   the spring onions.

MARCELLUS' CORN MUFFINS WITH WALNUT PRALINE CRUNCH

FOR THE MUFFINS

300g fine ground cornmeal

90g plain flour

1½ teaspoons baking powder

1 teaspoon bicarbonate of soda

1 teaspoon salt

1 egg

1½ teaspoons vanilla extract

45ml vegetable oil, plus extra
  for greasing

280ml buttermilk

80ml milk

FOR THE WALNUT PRALINE

100g granulated sugar

100g walnuts

MAKES 12

The Blue Grass Cook Book by a Minnie C. Fox (incredible name, to start) was published in 1904 and is composed almost entirely of recipes from Virginia or Kentucky. Packed full of achingly nostalgic and funny instructions, it's a real gem.

But the recipe that struck me most came from Marcellus. He is described as a sort of kitchen hand/cook and contributes a recipe for corn muffins. There isn't a picture of Marcellus but it isn't difficult to figure out that he was black, almost certainly an ex-slave himself or the son of a slave. Marcellus is given no surname, no real description, but it is blindingly obvious he was a phenomenal chef, if his recipe is anything to go by. I would like to try to honour a chef who didn't get much credit back in 1904. This recipe has been tweaked and altered, but it is most definitely Marcellus' creation.

----

❶ Preheat the oven to 180°C/gas mark 4. Pop 12 paper muffin cases into a deep muffin tin. Lightly grease a baking tray and set aside.

❷ To make the walnut praline, put the sugar and 1 tablespoon of cold water in a non-stick frying pan and melt over a medium heat until you achieve a rich caramel. Do NOT stir or you will crystallise it. Let it melt in its own time.

❸ Once you have a rich, brown caramel, pour in the walnuts and stir together briefly. Pour onto the baking tray and leave to cool. Once brittle, roughly chop the praline into chunks.

❹ For the muffins, put the cornmeal, flour, baking powder, bicarbonate of soda and salt in the bowl of a freestanding mixer and mix together well. Add the egg, vanilla, oil, buttermilk and milk and mix well. Scrape down to the bottom of the bowl occasionally to avoid lumps.

❺ Spoon the batter into the muffin cases (I use an ice-cream scoop – it helps to ensure portion control and if it has a self-scraping lever, even better). Sprinkle a handful of the praline on top of each muffin and bake for 25–30 minutes until risen, golden and firm. Best enjoyed cut in half and liberally buttered.

HAZELNUT CHOCOLATE TOASTER TARTS

FOR THE TOASTER TARTS

310g plain flour, plus extra for
    dusting

1 tablespoon caster sugar

1 teaspoon salt

220g cold salted butter, cut
    into 1cm cubes

2 eggs, lightly beaten

2 tablespoons milk

40g whole blanched hazelnuts

10 tablespoons Nutella

1 teaspoon sea salt flakes

1 tablespoon golden
    caster sugar

MAKES 5

I have very fond memories of toaster tarts. They were in my
school lunchbox and have never ceased to satisfy my late-night
cravings. And they are remarkably simple to make at home.

The most important thing is the pastry. You want a crisp,
thin, tender crumb that is strong enough to hold its own in a
toaster. I can't get enough of salt in sweet stuff, but by all
means play about with the fillings.

----

❶ Preheat the oven to 190°C/gas mark 5. Line two baking trays
with baking parchment.

❷ Put the flour, caster sugar and salt into a food processor
and blitz quickly together. Add the butter and blitz for
about 15 seconds until it resembles fine breadcrumbs.

❸ Tip the flour mixture into a bowl. Add half the beaten eggs
and all the milk, and mix using a cutlery knife until larger
chunks of pastry begin to form. Tip out onto a clean surface
and bring the pastry together by hand into a flat rectangle.
Wrap in clingfilm and chill for 10 minutes.

❹ Toast the hazelnuts in a dry pan until just coloured,
then roughly chop. Roll the pastry out on a lightly floured
surface to 3mm thick. Using a 9 x 13cm template, cut out
10 rectangles of pastry – I find a pizza wheel is easiest
for this.

❺ Place the rectangles on the prepared baking trays and prick
five of them with a fork. These will be the top of the tarts.
Chill for about 25 minutes until firm.

❻ To assemble the toaster tarts, spread 2 tablespoons of
Nutella per toaster tart on each unpricked pastry rectangle,
add a sprinkling of chopped nuts and a pinch of sea salt,
leaving a 1cm border. Brush the border with some of
remaining beaten egg and place the other half of the pop
tart on top, pricked-side up.

❼ Using a fork, press the edges together and trim off any
raggedy edges using the pizza wheel. Brush all over with the
egg and top with a dusting of golden caster sugar.

❽ Bake for 30–35 minutes until golden and crisp. Leave to cool
on a wire rack before attacking.

QUICK AND EASY CORNBREAD

FOR THE CORNBREAD

245g fine ground yellow cornmeal

75g plain flour

55g caster sugar

1 teaspoon salt

1½ teaspoons baking powder

2 eggs

380ml milk

90g unsalted butter,
  melted and cooled,
  plus extra for greasing

2 tablespoons runny honey

SERVES 8

I swear to God, the smell of freshly baked cornbread has to be the most comforting smell in the world. It's the baked version of Dorothy's three heel clicks. There's no place like home and there's no taste like cornbread. It's also ridiculously easy to make, so no excuses. If you're going to make chilli, by rights it comes with cornbread. So get to it!

---

❶ Preheat the oven to 180°C/gas mark 4. Grease and line a 20cm square baking tin with baking parchment.

❷ In a large mixing bowl, combine the cornmeal, flour, sugar, salt and baking powder, mixing well. In a separate jug, beat the eggs with the milk and melted butter.

❸ Gradually add the wet ingredients into the dry, making sure there are no dreaded lumps. Don't worry if the mixture looks very liquidy – it will do! Pour the mixture into the prepared tin. Bake for 35-40 minutes until light, risen and golden yellow.

❹ Remove the bread from the oven and stab it all over with a skewer, while still warm. Then drizzle all over with the honey and leave it to soak in. Slice the bread into 8 pieces (I go for triangles, but whatever floats your boat) and enjoy.

WHITE CHOCOLATE, CRANBERRY AND BLUEBERRY SCONES

FOR THE SCONES

310g plain flour, plus extra
   for dusting
2 tablespoons caster sugar
1 tablespoon baking powder
1 teaspoon salt
170g cold salted butter,
   cut into 1cm cubes
2 eggs, lightly beaten
135ml double cream
75g dried cranberries
75g dried blueberries
100g white chocolate chips
1 egg, lightly beaten,
   for glazing
1 tablespoon granulated sugar,
   for glazing

MAKES 8

When I was about thirteen years old, my dad and I went skiing in Stowe, Vermont, where for five days we lived in what I can only describe as my *Gilmore Girls* fantasy. The B&B we stayed in was heart-warmingly twee and the best thing about it was the scones. Triangular, enormous, lighter than air and packed with juicy, tangy bursts of blueberry.

❶ Preheat the oven to 190°C/gas mark 5. Line a baking tray with baking parchment.

❷ Put the flour, caster sugar, baking powder and salt in the bowl of a freestanding mixer and mix well. Add the butter and blend until the mixture resembles fine breadcrumbs.

❸ Whisk together the eggs and cream in a jug, then slowly pour this into the flour mixture. Tumble in the cranberries, blueberries and white chocolate chips, mixing only briefly. Don't overmix or you will break up the chips too much, so be tentative.

❹ Scrape the dough out onto a work surface dusted with flour. Knead it a few times, just to bring it together, and roll it into an 18cm diameter circle, 2-2.5cm thick. Transfer to the prepared baking tray. Using a sharp knife, cut the circle into eight wedges and glaze the top with the beaten egg. Sprinkle over the granulated sugar and bake for 30-35 minutes until light, golden and risen.

❺ Leave to cool on a wire rack before tearing apart along the cut lines into triangles. Serve with butter.

CHALLAH FRENCH TOAST WITH CARAMELISED APPLES AND WALNUTS

FOR THE FRENCH TOAST
----

2 eggs, lightly beaten
170ml milk
½ teaspoon vanilla extract
¼ teaspoon ground cinnamon
zest of ½ orange
good grating of whole nutmeg
pinch of salt
2 thick-cut slices of challah
30g salted butter

FOR THE APPLES AND WALNUTS

100g salted butter
100g caster sugar
2 eating apples, peeled,
   quartered and cored
50g walnut pieces

SERVES 2

This recipe uses challah — the classic Jewish bread, hence the recipe name — and the combination of apples and walnuts is a little nod to *charoset*, a typical mix of apples, nuts, sugar and spices eaten at Passover. Because of the lighter texture of the bread, the centre of the toast stays wonderfully squidgy and oozy, while the outside crisps up like a sunbather at Daytona.

----

❶ To make the French toast, whisk the eggs, milk, vanilla, cinnamon, orange zest, nutmeg and salt together in a shallow dish. Add the challah slices and leave to soak for about 5 minutes. The bread soaks up most of the liquid, so flip the slices over and allow to soak for a further 2 minutes.

❷ Melt the butter in a large frying pan and once foaming, add the challah slices. Cook over a medium heat for 2–3 minutes per side, or until dappled golden brown all over. Keep warm.

❸ For the apples and walnuts, melt the butter in a frying pan until foaming, then sprinkle in the sugar. Caramelise slightly, then add the apples and the walnut pieces. Cook for about 10 minutes, stirring occasionally, until the apples have softened nicely. Serve with the French toast.

PISTACHIO, HONEY AND GINGER GRANOLA

FOR THE GRANOLA

500g rolled oats

110g sesame seeds

160g ginger preserve

1 teaspoon ground cinnamon

1½ teaspoons ground ginger

100g golden syrup

100g soft light brown sugar

150g whole shelled pistachios, roughly chopped

100g whole almonds, roughly chopped

100g dried cranberries

100g dried figs, roughly chopped

80ml clear honey

1 teaspoon salt

4 tablespoons sunflower oil

Greek yogurt, to serve (optional)

strawberries, raspberries and blueberries, to serve (optional)

SERVES 8-10

Anyone that knows me knows, beyond any doubt, that any food labelled 'healthy' or 'raw' or even 'good for you' in *any* way sends me bolting in the other direction. I just can't do it. But, if you put loads of delicious nuts, fruits and spices in something supposedly 'better for you' than a bacon double cheeseburger and chilli fries, then I might just be tempted.

❶ Preheat the oven to 180°C/gas mark 4. Combine all the ingredients in a large mixing bowl. If the mixture looks a little dry, add an extra 1 tablespoon of honey at a time until it looks like slightly crumbly flapjack mix.

❷ Spread the mixture evenly over a large baking tray and bake for 20 minutes. Remove the tray from the oven and carefully stir the mixture using a spatula. You want a nice even golden colour.

❸ Return to the oven for a further 25–30 minutes. When it's done, the granola won't be particularly crunchy (this happens with cooling) but it will smell toasty and have a light brown colour. Leave to cool, then jar up. Serve with Greek yogurt, and fresh strawberries, raspberries and blueberries, if you like.

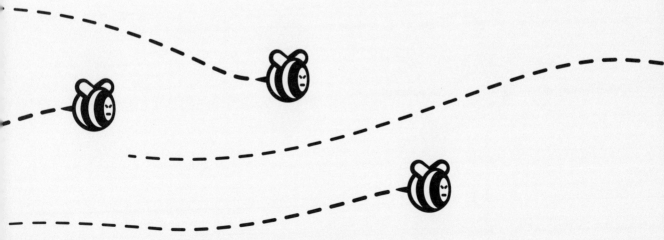

APPLE FRITTERS WITH GOAT'S CHEESE AND HONEY

FOR THE FRITTERS

310g plain flour

1 teaspoon bicarbonate
  of soda

2 tablespoons golden
  caster sugar

2 eggs, lightly beaten

240ml soured cream

4 tablespoons milk

30g salted butter,
  melted and cooled

5 medium Granny Smith apples,
  quartered and cored

2 teaspoons salt

750ml vegetable oil,
  for frying

150g soft goat's cheese

clear honey, for drizzling

MAKES 15-18

This recipe is based on one I found in *Early American Recipes* – a bunch of New England bites and dishes from, wait for it, 1953! I mean, one chapter is called 'Puddins & Pies' and, apparently, all the recipes are decidedly 'smackin' good'. If that is not 100 per cent adorable, then I have nothing to offer you.

----

❶ Sift the flour, bicarbonate of soda and caster sugar into a medium bowl.

❷ In a jug, mix together the eggs, soured cream, milk and melted butter until smooth. Make a well in the centre of the flour and pour in the wet mixture. Using a wooden spoon, gradually incorporate the flour into the wet ingredients by stirring very gently. If you do this too quickly, the mixture will be a lumpy, claggy mess, so be patient.

❸ Grate the apples coarsely, leaving the skins on, and sprinkle with the salt. Set aside for about 5 minutes, then squeeze out as much juice as possible, through a dry – and clean! – tea towel. Then add the grated apples to the batter and mix well.

❹ Pour the oil into a high-sided frying pan and heat gently. To test if it is ready to fry, plop in a little of the apple batter, and if it sizzles on the surface and turns golden and crisp within 30 seconds per side, you are good to go.

❺ Using two dessertspoons, carefully slide the fritters into the hot oil - you will probably need to work in batches. Once they are a rich golden colour on one side, carefully turn them using long tongs and cook on the other side.

❻ Drain the fritters on kitchen paper. To serve, take a spoonful of creamy goat's cheese and pile it on top of each fritter – be generous! Then drizzle with honey. Divine.

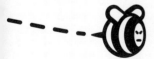

BURG

BARBECUE &

GERS,
SLOW
COOKING

I could easily eat a cheeseburger every day for the rest of my life and die a happy woman. There is something about a burger that has this weird, sorceress effect on me whereby I am utterly powerless to any form of decision-making or conviction. It's burger or nothing. I'm hopelessly devoted to a cheeseburger.

This is something of a love letter to the art of slow cooking, smoking, smothering and scorching. When I moved to London, having spent a chunk of my childhood living in Florida, I was horrified to find out that so many of the barbecues I went to, should really have been titled 'Tough Chewy Steak on a Stick Days'. Always, always, microscopic chicken drumsticks, limp lettuce or, the worst, utterly flavourless sausages, which I'm sure only qualified as such in the legal meat content sense.

I just couldn't get it. Why? When there is sweet, sticky chopped pork out there or Memphis dry-rub baby back ribs? Or real steaks?! Cooked until juicy and blushing in the middle like a young lover. It was just wrong.

What I love most about barbecue in its most original, down and dirty form (hot and steamy, covered in sauce and served in a basket for the whole family) is that it doesn't just reflect its roots, it's damn proud of them. Take my favourite, what would be my last meal on Earth and, frankly, what I want to be my last meal of every day: pulled pork. The recipes come pouring forward in their thousands when you ask for one. On a bus from Knoxville to Memphis, Tennessee, I got maybe twenty variations on the 'best darn way to tame that beast'.

Pork butt, always. Then start with a dry rub, massaging it into the grooves in the skin and all around the pink, soft flesh. You only need to sniff the heady, sultry mixture of paprika, garlic, cumin, coriander, Cajun spices and then heavy, molasses-rich brown sugar to know you are in for a treat. The braising liquid has to be sweet, to calm down the dry heat of the spices, but also tangy, to dance on your tongue. Both Alan and Ricky on the bus swore by apple juice, while beer braising is also popular, especially if you have your manhood to maintain. But my personal favourite white trash option? Straight-up Coca-Cola. Or if you come over all U.S. of A., then go for root beer. Slow, slow cook for as long as possible, six or seven hours at least, until it gives up the ghost and falls away from the bone with just a nudge of your fork. Then serve up, dig in, and never look back, with mac 'n' cheese, potato salad and endless napkins as your weapons at the ready.

As Dolly Parton said in *9 to 5*, 'I just love me some real barbecue'. And I do.

A note on barbecuing

- These recipes are intended for a coal burning, traditional barbecue. If using gas, simply follow the recipes and temper the heat as required.

- Preheat the barbecue *before* you start to cook.

- The method of heat (direct or indirect) is mentioned in each recipe.

Direct heat

- To cook using direct heat, spread the coals evenly over the basin of the barbecue and light. Leave the coals to heat until white hot, about 35–40 minutes, *before* you put any food on the grill.

- If using a gas barbecue, cook food over a high heat.

Indirect heat

- This method allows more gentle, controlled cooking. Pile the coals onto one side of the basin, leaving the other half empty. Light the coals and heat to glowing red hot, about 25–30 minutes.

- If using a gas barbecue, cook food over a moderate heat.

MEMPHIS DRY-RUB
BABY BACK RIBS

FOR THE RIBS

2 full racks pork baby back ribs (about 8–10 ribs per full rack)
3 heaped tablespoons Dijon mustard
1½ tablespoons ground cumin
1½ tablespoons ground coriander
1½ tablespoons smoked paprika
1½ tablespoons garlic powder
1½ tablespoons Cajun seasoning
1 teaspoon chilli powder
2 tablespoons soft dark brown sugar
1 teaspoon salt
good grinding of black pepper
350ml apple juice

TIP: If cooking this recipe in the oven, 30 minutes before the ribs are finished slow cooking, increase the heat to 220°C/gas mark 7 and remove the foil. Cook for 10 minutes uncovered, allowing the top to crisp up nicely.

SERVES 4

Apart from Graceland, Sun Studios and Johnny Cash, Memphis has reached global infamy for its ribs. I overheard a woman say to her friend 'Wet or dry, they're bonafide' – never a truer word said. The dry rub here gives the ribs a wonderfully smoky, earthy flavour, even if you are without a home smoker to prep them in. A half rack per person will fill you up nicely, but you'll have to strap your hands to your sides to stop stealing these little beauties off other people's plates.

❶ Remove that dang membrane on the back of the ribs by flipping the ribs so they are fleshy-side down and peeling off the thin layer of sinew on the back. This is easiest when they are cold so you can prize under the sinew with a cutlery knife if necessary.

❷ Put the ribs into a shallow roasting tray and smother with the mustard, rubbing it all over the racks. (It's important not to have the ribs overlapping because if you do, rather than being crispy, caramelised and deep golden brown when cooked, they will be flabby and a bit nasty.)

❸ In a bowl, mix together the spices, sugar and seasoning. Rub the spice mix all over the racks. At this point it's brilliant if you can leave the rub to do its thing. Keep the ribs marinating in the fridge for up to 48 hours and the flavour really seeps into the meat, but 30 minutes minimum will do if you're pressed for time.

❹ Preheat the oven to 150°C/gas mark 2. Pour the apple juice down the side of the roasting tray, not over the ribs otherwise you'll wash off the spices. Cover with foil.

❺ Slow cook the ribs in the oven for 4 hours. Then, 30 minutes before the ribs are done, spread the coals evenly over the basin of the barbecue and heat for 35–40 minutes until white hot. Remove the foil and cook the ribs straight on the hot barbecue for 5 minutes a side, letting the sugar become crispy and caramelly. Serve with Sweetheart, courgette and basil slaw (page 62), baked potatoes and soured cream.

JACK AND COKE PULLED PORK

FOR THE PULLED PORK

1 tablespoon cayenne pepper

1 tablespoon smoked paprika

1 tablespoon ground cumin

1 teaspoon garlic powder

1 teaspoon mustard powder

2 tablespoons soft dark
  brown sugar

1 tablespoon salt

good grinding of black pepper

2kg pork shoulder joint,
  with crackling

400ml Coca-Cola (not Diet)

150ml Jack Daniel's

2 tablespoons tomato purée

1 tablespoon cornflour

SERVES 4

Pulled pork is a Southern dinner staple, usually served with a dizzying amount of side dishes. Depending which part of the South you are from, your pulled pork defines you almost as much (or more so, in some cases) as your politics. This is serious stuff.

❶ Preheat the oven to 150°C/gas mark 2. Mix the spices, sugar, salt and black pepper together in a bowl. Set aside.

❷ Cut off any string that may be wrapped around the pork. Unfurl the meat and score the crackling with a small, sharp knife. Cut quite deeply as you really want the flavours to penetrate during cooking.

❸ Put the pork in a flameproof casserole and rub with the spices, half on top and into the fat, and half underneath into the flesh.

❹ Turn the pork skin-side up and pour the Coca-Cola and Jack Daniel's in around the edge. It looks like a lot of liquid, but it's just bubbles and will reduce during cooking.

❺ Cover the casserole with foil, then put on the lid and cook for at least 6 hours. Low and slow wins the race here. Baste the pork while it cooks, but not too often – ladle the sweet braising liquid over the meat every 2 hours if you wish.

❻ Remove from the oven, take the pork out of the casserole and place onto a plate. Remove the fatty layer from the top and discard, then shred the pork using two forks. Cover with foil and set aside while you make the sauce.

❼ Whisk the tomato purée into the braising liquid. Then, over a very high heat, start to reduce the liquid by bringing it to a forceful boil, with the lid off. Check the seasoning, and then mix the cornflour with 2 tablespoons of cold water and pour into the sauce. Whisk well and leave to thicken to a nice gravy-like quality.

❽ Plate up the pork and pour a little sauce over the top. Decant the remaining sauce into a jug so that diners can devour it. Best served with Ruby-red slaw (page 62) and chased with a Mint julep (page 164).

GRILLED BUFFALO STEAK WITH PICKLED BLUEBERRY SAUCE

FOR THE STEAK

----

1 x 400g buffalo rump steak
drizzle of olive oil
1 garlic clove, peeled
200g blueberries
4 tablespoons red wine vinegar
1 tablespoon whiskey
1 tablespoon redcurrant jelly
salt, to taste
freshly ground black pepper,
   to taste

SERVES 2

Native American food is American food in its most authentic form and it's only right to reflect that. Buffalo and bison (which are a little leaner and slightly more irony in flavour than beef) were the original meat-producing animals before beef cattle came on the scene and are fairly readily available these days. The blueberries here provide a wonderfully sharp twist that cuts through that intense meatiness. This is my nod to the unmatchable natural produce of the USA.

----

❶ Spread the coals evenly over the basin of the barbecue and heat for 35–40 minutes until white hot.

❷ Meanwhile, lay the steak in a shallow dish, drizzle with olive oil and rub with the garlic. Cover with clingfilm and set aside.

❸ Next, make the sauce by placing the blueberries, red wine vinegar, whiskey and redcurrant jelly in a small saucepan. Mix together and bring to a gentle simmer. Stir regularly to stop any sticking and burning, and cook for about 10 minutes with the lid off, until the sauce has reduced down fully and is thick, sticky and deep-violet in colour.

❹ Season the steak well and grill for 2 minutes each side if you want it rare, or 4–5 minutes a side if you like it medium. Anything more does not bear thinking about. Remove the steak from the heat and leave it to rest for at least 10 minutes. Slice it into strips and serve with Blackened corn on the cob – All dressed up (page 61).

BEER AND JUNIPER-BRAISED BEEF BRISKET

FOR THE BRISKET

2 tablespoons vegetable oil

1.5kg beef brisket

salt and freshly ground black pepper, to taste

2 heaped tablespoons Dijon mustard

75g soft dark brown sugar

1 tablespoon juniper berries

1 tablespoon fennel seeds

440ml beer

2 bay leaves

2 tablespoons liquid smoke

sprig of fresh rosemary

SERVES 4-6

This dish is the poster child of slow cooking – tender, yielding and unctuous, with flavours that just melt into each other. Brisket is similar to pork or lamb shoulder in that it does a lot of work on the animal so needs to be cooked low and slow to break down all the connective tissue developed by moving around so much. Beer, beef and aromatic herbs were made to go together, as I hope this shows. This is even better the day after you cook it and makes a heavenly taco or sandwich filler.

❶ Preheat the oven to 160°C/gas mark 3. Heat the oil in a large flameproof casserole and season the brisket all over. Brown the brisket on all sides over a high heat, then transfer to a plate and leave to rest for a few minutes.

❷ While the beef is still warm, brush it with the mustard and roll in the sugar. Toast the juniper berries and fennel seeds lightly in a dry frying pan and add to the casserole.

❸ Return the beef to the casserole and pour the beer in around the sides. Pop in the bay leaves, liquid smoke and rosemary, and cover with foil before firmly placing the lid back on top. Cook in the oven for 6–8 hours.

❹ When the time comes, carefully remove the brisket from the braising liquid and shred it using two forks, or even your hands if it's not too hot. (You could drizzle a few tablespoons of the braising liquor over the meat before serving, if you like.) Delicious right away, this is even more delightful after a day or two, so if you are a planner, cook in advance and reheat in the oven to serve.

REAL TEXAN CHILLI

FOR THE CHILLI

3 tablespoons vegetable oil

650g beef braising steak, cut into 3cm cubes

salt and freshly ground black pepper, to taste

5 rashers smoked streaky bacon, cut into lardon-size pieces

1 large onion, finely diced

2 garlic cloves, crushed

1½ teaspoons chilli powder

1 teaspoon ground cumin

1 teaspoon ground coriander

1 teaspoon smoked hot paprika

90ml strong black coffee

340ml beer

400g can chopped tomatoes

2 tablespoons tomato purée

1 cinnamon stick

2 bay leaves

3 red peppers, core and seeds removed, cut into 2cm cubes

2 teaspoons caster sugar

TO SERVE

150ml soured cream

100g strong Cheddar cheese, coarsely grated

5 spring onions, finely sliced

SERVES 4-6

There are a million different chilli recipes and variations across the United States, with each one declaring to be the 'original', the 'best' or even the 'true' chilli. From my experience, and for ease, there are two broad types of chilli con carne: Soup style and Texas style.

Soup style is what you will most often come across, made from minced beef, cooked until quite loose with lots of tomatoes and kidney beans. Texas style is made with chunks of braising steak with not a bean in sight. Apparently, there is a saying in Texas that goes, 'We got a lot of beef but not many beans', making chilli much more of a meaty casserole.

Chilli was supposedly the original ready meal – cowboys doing long trips with their cattle would pack dried bricks of chilli to reheat with water over a fire. Into this pot they would often throw the remains of their coffee, giving the whole stew a subtle richness. While the dried brick thing is a little bit of a stretch for the modern diet, the coffee thing I'll go for and think it makes this chilli something special. A nod of the Stetson to the cowboys of the past.

❶ Preheat the oven to 160°C/gas mark 3. Heat the vegetable oil in a large flameproof casserole and season the braising steak well. Brown the steak in batches and place on a lipped plate, to keep hold of all the juices.

❷ In the same casserole, fry the bacon until most of the fat has rendered off and then add the onion and garlic. Sauté for about 5 minutes until just starting to colour. Add the chilli powder, cumin, coriander and paprika, and fry for 1 minute.

❸ Pour in the coffee to deglaze the pan, scraping off all the tasty bits that may have stuck to the bottom. Add the beer and bring to the boil, then reduce to a simmer.

❹ Add the chopped tomatoes, tomato purée, cinnamon stick, bay leaves, red peppers and sugar and mix well. Return the steak to the dish, pouring in all the juicy goodness that may have seeped out while resting. Cover with foil, then the lid and cook for 3 hours in the oven.

❺ Remove the cinnamon stick and bay leaves and serve with a dollop of soured cream, a sprinkling of cheese, some spring onions and a whole lot of love.

PEANUT BUTTER AND BACON BURGERS

FOR THE BURGERS

500g minced beef chuck steak
1½ teaspoons garlic powder
½ teaspoon onion powder
¼ teaspoon mustard powder
salt and freshly ground black
    pepper, to taste
good grating of whole nutmeg
1 tablespoon vegetable oil

TO SERVE
----

8 rashers unsmoked streaky
    bacon
4 good-quality burger buns
30g salted butter, melted
8 heaped tablespoons chunky
    peanut butter
4 large leaves of cos lettuce
½ small red onion, finely sliced

SERVES 4

Peanut butter and bacon are two of my desert island
foodstuffs, so when I saw that a bar in New Orleans served
them on a burger, there was no way I wasn't going to try it.
But when we arrived at Yo Mama's Bar and Grill, it seemed less
like a rough-and-ready, home-cooking restaurant and more like,
well, a strip club. We couldn't see the exact colour of our
food because of the red lights.

While we looked awkwardly away from the bare-buttocked
mannequin that hung over the bathroom door, we tucked into
what was, and still is, one of the best burgers I've ever had.
The flavours take on this satay-like sweet/salty divinity that
is ideal in a burger.

----

❶ To make the burgers, put the mince, garlic, onion and
mustard powders, salt, black pepper and nutmeg in a large
bowl. Mix well with your hands, then divide the mixture into
four equal-sized balls. Throw each ball, one at a time,
between your hands with force five or six times, a bit like
you are playing catch with yourself. This helps the patties
hold their shape. Then form each one into a disc about 1.5cm
thick and refrigerate.

❷ Preheat the oven to 200°C/gas mark 6. Spread the coals
evenly over the basin of the barbecue and heat for
35–40 minutes until white hot. Brush each patty with
the oil. Grill for about 3 minutes per side if you like it
pink in the middle, or a few minutes longer for well done.

❸ Spread the bacon rashers out flat and sandwich them between
two baking trays. Cook in the oven for 4–6 minutes until
crispy, checking regularly so they don't burn. Remove from
the trays and set aside.

❹ Split the buns in half and brush the insides with the melted
butter. Spread 2 heaped tablespoons of peanut butter on top
of each patty and top with 2 rashers of bacon. Dress the
burgers with the lettuce and onion, and devour.

HOME-SMOKED HOT LINKS WITH DIXIE PEACH SALSA

FOR THE HOT LINKS

45g fine wood chips (I like
  to use maple or apple wood
  because they are naturally
  sweeter)
1 tablespoon vegetable oil
4 Cumberland sausages
4 hot dog buns
20g salted butter, melted

FOR THE SALSA

3 large peaches, stones removed
  and diced into 1cm cubes
1 red chilli, deseeded and
  finely chopped
juice and zest of 1 lime
2 tablespoons extra virgin
  olive oil
a small handful of fresh mint,
  finely chopped
a small handful of fresh
  coriander, finely chopped
salt and freshly ground black
  pepper, to taste

SERVES 4

Stove-top hot smoking is ridiculously easy and elevates
something pretty normal and everyday into something so full-
bodied and punchy it's like a fine, old wine. Except meatier.

Hot smoking is based around heat so is actually cooking your
food as you go, unlike cold smoking where you still have to
put some heat to it. So, these links aka sausages will be
cooked almost all the way through by the time they are done
in the smoker, meaning they just require a flash on the grill
for some nice, charred caramelisation. The hardest part of
home smoking is choosing what wood chips to use. Maple or
apple wood have a syrupy sweetness, while hickory gives you
a strong, earthy tone. I'm just waiting for the day you can
mix and match your own blends, like in fancy coffee shops.

❶ Build your stove-top smoker. This is really easy — take a
  large, high-sided pan (like a stockpot) that you don't mind
  staining a bit, and line the bottom with a double layer of
  foil. Sprinkle the wood chips onto the middle of the foil
  and place a steamer directly over the wood chips. Brush the
  steam trivet lightly with the oil and place the sausages on
  it, leaving space between each one for the heat to
  circulate. Spread the coals evenly over the basin of the
  barbecue and heat for 35–40 minutes until white hot.

❷ Cover the smoking pan with foil and cook the sausages over
  a high heat until you start to see smoke escaping from the
  edges. Place the lid firmly on top and reduce the heat to
  low. Cook for 10–12 minutes, depending on the thickness
  of your sausages.

❸ Meanwhile, make the salsa. Mix together the peaches, chilli,
  lime juice and zest, oil, mint, coriander, salt and black
  pepper in a bowl. Warm the hot dog buns up nicely, split
  them in half and brush the insides with melted butter.

❹ Once the sausages are cooked, remove carefully from the
  smoker and finish off on the barbecue to get a nice
  caramelisation on the outside. Serve in the buns, topped
  with the salsa.

SMOKY PORK BURGERS

FOR THE BURGERS

500g lean pork mince

1 small eating apple, cored
   and coarsely grated

4 rashers smoked streaky bacon,
   cut into small lardon-
   sized pieces

1 teaspoon wholegrain mustard

good grating of whole nutmeg

¾ teaspoon liquid smoke

½ teaspoon salt

¼ teaspoon freshly ground
   black pepper

1 tablespoon vegetable oil

TO SERVE

4 good-quality burger buns

30g salted butter, melted

4 large leaves of Cos lettuce

1 beefsteak tomato, sliced

½ small red onion, finely sliced

SERVES 4

One of the biggest challenges if you want to cook real Southern barbecue is smoking. Unless you've got a purpose-built smoker (I think I'm safe in saying this is unlikely), it can be tricky to get that intense muskiness. So, meet my secret weapon – liquid smoke. The inventors – or *geniuses* – of this treat smoke in the same way as distillers treat gin or vodka. They heat the wood of choice, then trap the vapours and rapidly cool them, bottling the result and providing you and me with a taste of true barbecue, with minimal effort.

The fat from the streaky bacon rashers helps baste the burgers from inside, so the pork doesn't get overly dry and grainy as you grill it. Juicy, smoky, tender – just how it should be.

❶ To make the burgers, put the mince, grated apple, bacon, mustard, nutmeg, liquid smoke, salt and black pepper into a large bowl. Mix well with your hands, then pull off four even-sized balls. Throw each ball, one at a time, between your hands with force five or six times, a bit like you are playing catch with yourself. This helps the patties hold their shape. Then form each one into a disc about 1.5cm thick and refrigerate.

❷ Spread the coals evenly over the basin of the barbecue and heat for 35–40 minutes until white hot. Brush each patty lightly with the oil. Grill for about 3 minutes per side until cooked through.

❸ Split the buns in half and brush the insides with the melted butter. Serve the burgers dressed with the lettuce, tomato and onion, and a healthy pile of fries.

DOUBLE CHEESEBURGERS

FOR THE BURGERS
----

1 quantity of burger recipe
  (Peanut butter and bacon
  burgers, page 53)
8 slices of cheese (any cheese
  you like best: American sliced
  is great for authenticity,
  or Swiss melts beautifully)

TO SERVE
----

4 good-quality burger buns
30g salted butter, melted
4 large leaves of Cos lettuce
1 beefsteak tomato, sliced
½ small red onion, finely
  sliced
4 dill pickles, sliced
  lengthways

SERVES 4

A double cheeseburger would be my last meal on Earth. I've
eaten more cheeseburgers than my arteries care to remember,
but what I've learnt over the years is the best ones leave
the meat alone: a little seasoning and that's it. No eggs,
breadcrumbs, parsley. Nada. The trick is to get great-quality
meat because that takes care of the bulk of the hard work
for you.

----

❶ Make the burger patties (see page 53). Divide the mixture
  into eight small equal-sized balls and then shape into discs
  about 1cm thick. Chill in the fridge.

❷ Spread the coals over the basin of the barbecue and heat
  for 25–30 minutes until red hot, then pile the coals onto
  one side of the basin. Brush each patty lightly with the
  oil. Grill the patties for about 2 minutes per side, on the
  side above the hot coals. Once flipped, gather the patties
  to the coal-less side, top each with a slice of cheese and
  cover with the lid. This helps to generate some steam,
  causing the cheese to melt.

❸ Split the buns in half and lightly toast on the hot side
  of the grill. Brush the insides with the melted butter.
  Pile high with the lettuce, tomato, onion and pickles.

❹ Stack two patties on top of each other, cheesy-side up,
  and slip into the buns. Serve immediately. Consume with joy.

CIDER CAN CHICKEN

FOR THE CHICKEN

440ml can of cider

1 whole medium chicken,
weighing about 1.8kg,
giblets removed

1 teaspoon garlic powder

1 teaspoon ground cumin

1 teaspoon ground coriander

1 teaspoon cayenne pepper

1 tablespoon fennel seeds

1½ teaspoons smoked sweet
paprika

1 tablespoon salt

freshly ground black pepper,
to taste

3 tablespoons vegetable oil

70ml treacle

40ml maple syrup

SERVES 4

I can't even begin to tell you how brilliant a way of cooking chicken this is. This method is foolproof. The liquid from the cider can constantly evaporates into the bird, meaning you would be hard-pressed to have dry breast meat at the end of it. I'm not saying you couldn't, but you would have to try really, *really* hard.

For the best of both worlds, I cook the chicken in the oven and finish it on the barbecue grill for that lovely charred taste. This also means that you can cook the chicken in advance, put it in the fridge and grill it when you want.

❶ Preheat the oven to 190°C/gas mark 5. Pour out half the can of cider (or drink it!). Line a large roasting tray with foil and stand the can in the centre.

❷ Prepare the chicken by cutting off the parson's nose and any excess skin that may be left around the neck cavity. Cut two deep slashes diagonally across the drumsticks and shimmy the chicken onto the cider can so that the breast is facing you and the wings are on top. It should look like the chicken is standing up and waving at you.

❸ In a small bowl, mix together the garlic powder, cumin, coriander, cayenne, fennel seeds, paprika, salt and black pepper. Brush the chicken with the oil, then rub in the spices. Drop some down into the cavity so the flavours really permeate while cooking. Cook for 1 hour.

❹ Meanwhile, spread the coals evenly over the basin of the barbecue and heat for 35–40 minutes until white hot.

❺ In a small bowl, mix together the treacle and maple syrup. Carefully remove the chicken from the oven and ease it off the cider can. Brush with the treacle–maple mix and then whack it straight onto the hot grill. It will char and go gorgeously caramelly. Grill for about 10 minutes until nicely scorched, then carve and serve.

BLACKENED CORN ON THE COB – ALL DRESSED UP

FOR THE CORN ON THE COB
----

1 tablespoon salt
4 corn on the cob, husks
  discarded
2 tablespoons vegetable oil

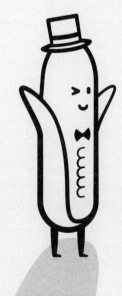

SERVES 4 (AS A SIDE)

Corn is quite a forgiving vegetable. It can take being blackened and charred, and yet still be juicy and tender. Like everything in life, it is better with butter. But rather than just sticking with the same old salty set-up, why not give one of these flavoured jobbies a go? You don't want to wear the same outfit to every party you go to, right? Well neither does your corn!

----

❶ Add the salt to a large pan of water and bring to the boil. Spread the coals evenly over the basin of the barbecue and heat for 35–40 minutes until white hot.

❷ Boil the corn cobs for 20 minutes. The kernels will still feel firm, but they will soften as they dry a little. Remove from the pan with tongs and drain on kitchen paper.

❸ Brush the corn with the oil and place on the grill. Turn regularly, making sure they transform into dappled gold and black. Smother in a topping of your choice to serve. Have napkins at the ready.

ORANGE AND MAPLE BUTTER (ENOUGH FOR 4 CORN ON THE COB)

Blend 100g softened salted butter, the zest of 1 orange, a pinch of smoked sweet paprika and 1½ teaspoons of maple syrup in a food processor until smooth. Serve straight away or store in an airtight container in the fridge for up to a month.

FIERY GREEN BUTTER

Blend 100g softened salted butter, 2 crushed garlic cloves, 1 whole green chilli, a small handful of fresh coriander (stalks included), roughly chopped, and a 3cm piece of peeled and grated root ginger, in a food processor until smooth. Serve straight away or store in an airtight container in the fridge for up to 2 weeks.

CAYENNE AND LIME SOURED CREAM

Mix together 95g soured cream, the zest of ½ lime, ½ teaspoon of cayenne pepper, salt and black pepper in a small bowl and serve.

SLAWS

TIP: All slaws last for
at least one day if covered
and refrigerated, but toss
them with some form of
acidic liquid such as lemon
juice or white wine vinegar
to stop them going brown
and sad.

Coleslaw comes from the Dutch word 'koolsla' meaning 'cabbage salad' and supposedly became a staple of the pan-American diet due to the need for impoverished Dutch immigrants to make ends meet. I define slaw as any salad that uses raw, shredded cabbage as the base. So thanks, Dutch people!

ORANGE, FENNEL AND WHITE BALSAMIC SLAW

❶ Put 2 oranges, peeled, pith removed and cut into segments (frames reserved for juice) in a small bowl and set aside. Squeeze the orange juice out of the remaining orange 'frame' into a separate bowl for the dressing.

❷ Put ½ head of white cabbage, core removed and finely shredded, 2 sticks of celery, finely sliced on the diagonal, and 2 fennel bulbs, quartered, core removed and finely shredded, into a large bowl.

❸ Now for the dressing: gradually add 4 tablespoons of rapeseed oil to the orange juice, whisking constantly. It should thicken slightly and turn a vibrant, sunset orange. Arrange the orange segments on top and serve in big portions.

SWEETHEART, COURGETTE AND BASIL SLAW

❶ Put 1 sweetheart cabbage, core removed and finely shredded, into a large bowl and add 2 banana shallots, finely sliced into half moons, and 4 courgettes, sliced into matchsticks. Cut a large handful of fresh basil into thin strips and add.

❷ Mix together 280ml soured cream, juice of 1 lemon, salt and white pepper in a jug. Pour over the slaw and mix well.

RUBY-RED SLAW

❶ Mix together ½ red cabbage, core removed and finely shredded, 1 red onion, finely sliced into half moons, 110g pomegranate seeds, 4 beetroots, peeled and cut into matchsticks, and 3 carrots, peeled and coarsely grated, in a bowl.

❷ Whisk together 100ml extra virgin olive oil, 2 tablespoons of pomegranate molasses, 3 tablespoons of red wine vinegar, salt and black pepper, and pour over the slaw. Using your hands, massage it all together. Finish off with a large handful of roughly chopped fresh flat-leaf parsley.

BBQ SPRING ONIONS WITH ROSEMARY AND HAZELNUT BUTTER

FOR THE SPRING ONIONS

6 spring onions

1 tablespoon vegetable oil

50g whole blanched hazelnuts

75g salted butter

¼ teaspoon cayenne pepper

¼ teaspoon grated whole nutmeg

½ tablespoon finely chopped
   fresh rosemary

salt and freshly ground black
   pepper, to taste

SERVES 2 (AS A SIDE)

When spring onions languish on the hot rods of a barbecue grill for long enough, that sharp, acrid, passion-killing juice gets transformed into a sweet, smoky nectar that cannot be oversold. They are irresistible when treated well – and dousing them in butter and rosemary doesn't hurt either.

---

❶ Spread the coals evenly over the basin of the barbecue and heat for 35–40 minutes until white hot.

❷ Trim the hairy end off the spring onions and give them a really good wash. You can trim a little of the green off the top too, but you want to keep them nice and long. Dry well with kitchen paper.

❸ Brush the onions lightly with the vegetable oil and place straight onto the grill. You want them to soften, turning limp and juicy while still taking on some decent colour, so cook for 6–8 minutes.

❹ Meanwhile, toast the hazelnuts in a dry pan until brown. Tip onto a board and roughly chop – you want to keep them fairly chunky. Leave the pan to cool a little before adding the butter, cayenne and nutmeg and returning to the heat.

❺ Let the butter melt, go foamy and start to turn just a touch brown before removing from the heat and adding the rosemary, salt, black pepper and nuts.

❻ To serve, arrange the spring onions in a pile on a large platter and spoon the nutty, aromatic, enticing butter all over the top.

TIP: This recipe is the base of a fab couscous or rice salad. Follow the instructions above, but use the butter as a dressing, stirred through the couscous or rice once cooked, and chop the onions into bite-sized pieces for easy forking.

GRILLED BROCCOLI WITH OREGANO AND CRISPY GARLIC

FOR THE BROCCOLI

1 head of broccoli, cut into florets

100ml olive oil

3 garlic cloves, thinly sliced

a small bunch of fresh oregano, finely chopped

salt and freshly ground black pepper, to taste

SERVES 4 (AS A SIDE)

If you are going to grill, you might as well try to grill everything. Nothing is impossible when it comes to barbecue. People said Wilbur and Orville Wright couldn't fly a plane, and they did just that. I like to think the same people said that about barbecuing veggies, and just look what we have here!

This is not a dish to choose if you have a hot date coming over — but in any other circumstance, then dive right in.

❶ Spread the coals evenly over the basin of the barbecue and heat for 35–40 minutes until white hot. Bring a large pan of salted water to the boil.

❷ Blanch the broccoli florets for 2 minutes until the stalks are just tender. Then plunge immediately into a bowl of iced water to stop them cooking further and set their vibrant green colour. Drain and pat dry using kitchen paper.

❸ Gently heat the olive oil in a shallow frying pan: you don't want it to burn, so don't whack it on full blast just yet. Add the garlic and cook until the edges just start to turn golden — they will continue cooking off the heat. Remove the pan immediately from the heat, let the oil cool a little, then add the oregano while still warm. Season to taste and set aside.

❹ Making sure the florets are really dry (otherwise they will just steam), place them onto the grill and cook for about 30 seconds on each side until gloriously charred. Transfer to a serving dish and dress liberally with the garlicky, herby oil.

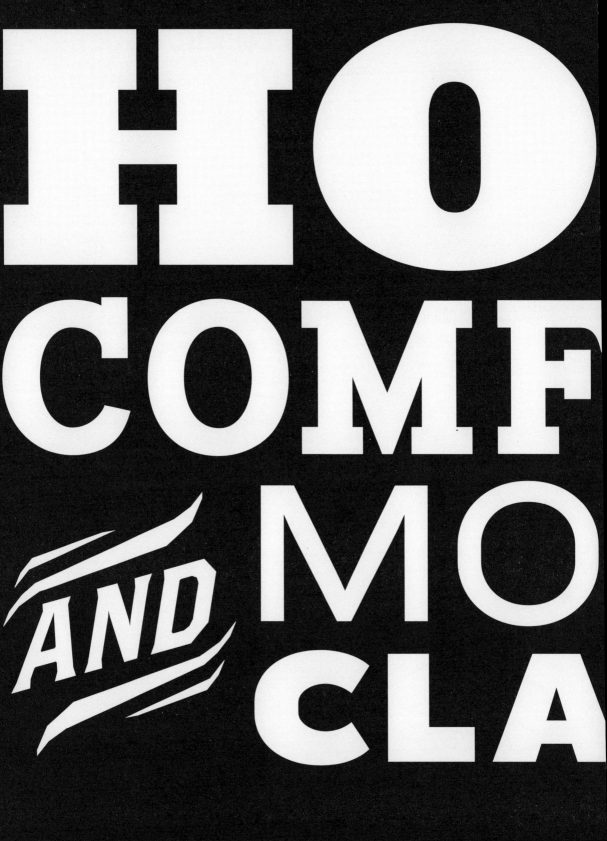

ME

F-

ORTS

DERN

SSICS

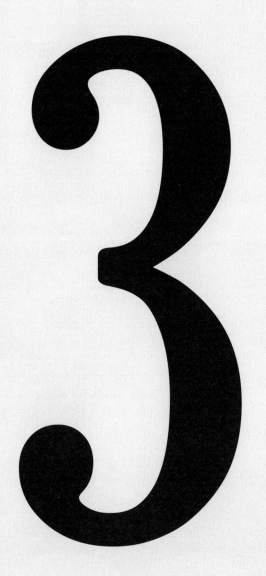

Sometimes all I want is a soft pretzel and a lemonade. Some people want flashy holidays where a mini bar is non-negotiable and poolside service comes as standard, but all I need is a twisted bundle of dough and something sharp to wash it down with.

A few years ago my mum and I took a trip to New York over New Year's. I'd been to the Big Apple before but always in spring or summer and as a sucker for Nora Ephron movies, I wanted to re-imagine my suburban, London life as an extra in, oh I don't know, *You've Got Mail*. The second we stepped off the plane my toes turned blue and I took out shares in Starbucks' Hot Apple Cider. It. Was. Freaking. Freezing. I mean – C.O.L.D. One night, I had to stand (not wash... stand still) under a hot shower just to defrost.

So after our blood-sugar levels had spiked from drinking enough caramel lattes and whipped cream hot chocolates to send a small village into cardiac arrest, the one thing I craved was salt. I don't really have a sweet tooth, but after wandering around in Central Park freezing our tuckus's off, the Lord best find me a pretzel fast. And he did. Crusty, thick, doughy and crystalline, with tiny bursts of salt just to keep you on your toes. It was like I had come home, just by chomping on that pretzel.

Home cooking is exactly this. It's the edible equivalent of a duvet and four pillows. It makes you feel warm inside, happy outside and puts you to sleep in about three seconds. If you've ever tried to have a productive day after a humongous bowl of chicken parmesan – gooooood luck, my friend. I'll see you in sleepy town. Population: 2.

There are some dishes that are so ubiquitous in the American kitchen – and especially the home kitchen, the kitchen with memories of chocolate-stained aprons and burnt fingers from stealing from the baking tray – that they deserve real recognition. These are the foods that got you through your childhood, teen years, and if you're anything like me, most weeknights of your adult life. They are familiar and friendly (or at least they will be with these recipes). They are the stuff we cook without even thinking about it; they are HEROES. These dishes will save your life. Tell me a time you have been wandering through the aisles of a supermarket at about 7pm on a Wednesday mulling over 'something to have for dinner that's quick and easy but I really can't justify pizza for the third night in a row'. (Just for the record, you TOTALLY can, but I hear you friends, we have some standards to maintain.) If this is you – lonely food forager finding no solace in the frozen ready-meal section – I'm with you. And more importantly, these recipes are with you. The beauties you'll find in this chapter are almost all one of these magic three things: easy, quick or irresistible.

WHISKEY MOLASSES-GLAZED BAKED HAM

FOR THE HAM

1.4kg boneless gammon joint
1 large white onion, quartered
1 tablespoon whole black
  peppercorns
1 tablespoon cloves
95g blackstrap molasses
20ml whiskey, preferably bourbon

SERVES 6

The term 'blackstrap molasses' has to be one of my all-time favourites. It is so achingly spot-on, you can almost imagine people using it to varnish leather straps or steel-cap boots. It's strong, punchy and unapologetically direct – exactly like molasses themselves. The 'strap' part comes from the Dutch word 'stroop' meaning syrup and black, well that's pretty self-explanatory.

One of my favourite antique cookbooks from 1904 features a guest recipe for a baked ham from one Col. W. M. Rhodes Estill who *starts* the method by stating 'kill your hogs when the wind is from the north west'. I'll spare you this step and give you the 'express' version instead. This ham is divine eaten right away while hot or, if you want to serve it in the most traditional, Kentucky way, leave it to cool completely. It makes for insanely good sandwiches.

----

❶ Line a roasting tray with foil. Put the gammon in a large pan and cover with cold water. Add the onion, peppercorns and cloves, and bring to the boil. Reduce the heat to a strong simmer and cook, uncovered, for 45 minutes.

❷ Preheat the oven to 190°C/gas mark 5. Remove the ham from the water (keep this, it makes a great base for a ham soup with the leftovers), pat dry with kitchen paper and place in the prepared roasting tray.

❸ In a small bowl, mix together the molasses and whiskey, then brush all over the ham. Don't use all the glaze as you will need to re-glaze during cooking.

❹ Roast for 20 minutes, then re-glaze. Roast for a further 20 minutes before glazing a third and final time before a last 20 minutes cooking. In total, the ham should be in the oven for 1 hour.

❺ Leave the ham to rest for 10 minutes before carving into thin strips. Best served with well-buttered baked potatoes and a vast array of chutneys and pickles.

CLASSIC BEEF
POT ROAST

3 tablespoons vegetable oil

salt and freshly ground black
  pepper, to taste

1 x 1.8kg chuck eye roll
  (also called 'beef chuck
  pot roast' or 'beef chuck
  slow roast')

5 large carrots, peeled and
  cut into 4cm chunks

12 shallots, peeled

560ml Californian Shiraz

300ml hot beef stock

1 tablespoon juniper berries

1 tablespoon whole black
  peppercorns

2 bay leaves

sprig of fresh rosemary

a small bunch of fresh thyme

SERVES 8

If you can't do a roast, do pot roast. This is a really slow-cooked, braised chuck of beef, which is the muscle group just above the neck. Perfect if you like to have a lot of what I call 'allotted panic time'. If your side dishes aren't quite there and people are milling in slower than a Greyhound bus on a national holiday, and you haven't set the table in the same way the Barefoot Contessa did – don't worry. The beef is more than happy to sit in the oven, jacuzzi-ing away in the herb-spiked red-wine broth. Pot roast was made for Sundays and lazy people. My fellow couch lovers – it was made for us.

❶ Heat most of the oil in a large flameproof casserole (big enough to hold the beef, all the veggies *and* liquid) to a high heat and preheat the oven to 150°C/gas mark 2. Season the meat well all over and then sear on each side. You want a really lovely, rich, deep-brown colour to add a depth of flavour to the final roast.

❷ Once browned, remove the beef and set aside on a plate. Deglaze the pan with a splash of cold water. If there are any black bits lingering at the bottom, scrape them off and discard. Add a dash more oil and heat again, this time browning the carrots and then the shallots in two separate batches so as not to crowd the pan.

❸ Remove the veggies, set aside on a plate and add the wine to the pan. Boil off the raw alcohol flavour and once it's reduced by about one-third, add the stock, juniper berries, peppercorns, bay leaves, rosemary and thyme.

❹ Place the beef carefully in the middle of the pot, pouring in any juices from the plate. Arrange the vegetables around him and cover with a sheet of foil, then a tight-fitting lid. Transfer to the oven and cook the pot roast for 4 hours.

❺ To check the meat is ready, it should just fall apart when poked gently with a fork or spoon. If it is, very carefully remove it from the pot and slice as best you can – remember it's rustic.

TIP: Like most casseroles, or fine wines, this gets better with a little age. You can make this the day before, leaving the beef in the broth and wine, and simply reheat to serve. It will be even more tender and rich.

CHICKEN PARMESAN

FOR THE CHICKEN

150g dried pasta (I like to
   use trompetti or strozzapreti)
2 chicken breasts, skinless
70ml vegetable oil
80g plain flour
3 eggs, lightly beaten
120g panko breadcrumbs
20g Parmesan cheese, grated,
   plus Parmesan shavings,
   to serve

FOR THE SAUCE

1 tablespoon olive oil
1 medium white onion,
   finely diced
1 garlic clove, crushed
400g can cherry tomatoes
1 tablespoon tomato purée
90ml red wine
1 teaspoon caster sugar
salt and freshly ground black
   pepper, to taste
a large handful of fresh basil,
   roughly torn

SERVES 2

The first and most important thing you should know about this is its pronunciation. CHICKEN (easy enough) PAR-MEH-JAHN. A distinct 'jjj' sound on the last syllable is paramount.

This is essentially a chicken schnitzel, jazzed up with some Parmesan and slipped onto a big ole' bowl of steaming, hot, rich, sweet, tomatoey pasta. It's risky, though, because of how relatively easy it is to make. You can get some *reeeally* awful ones: dry, dull, soggy, bland. But the simplicity of this dish means you can also get it so spot on. Just pay attention to your tomato sauce. Don't take this for granted like an overlooked boyfriend. Value it, give it time and, like all good men, a little seasoning.

❶ Start by making the sauce. Heat the oil in a small saucepan and sweat the onion, covered with a piece of damp baking parchment, for about 10 minutes until really soft.

❷ Add the garlic and cook for about another minute until aromatic. Tip in the cherry tomatoes, tomato purée, wine, sugar, salt and black pepper, and bring to the boil. Reduce the heat to a simmer and cook for 20 minutes, stirring occasionally.

❸ For the chicken, boil a large pan of water for the pasta, generously seasoned with salt. Add the pasta and cook for 7 minutes, until just al dente.

❹ Place the chicken breasts, one at a time, between two sheets of baking parchment and beat using a rolling pin to about 1cm thick. Trim off any straggly bits around the edge and set aside.

❺ Heat the oil in a high-sided frying pan and measure out the flour into one bowl, season well, put the beaten eggs into another bowl and the panko and grated Parmesan into a third. Dip the chicken first in the flour, then the egg and finally the breadcrumbs.

❻ Fry the chicken in the hot oil for about 2 minutes per side, until golden brown and cooked all the way through.

❼ Drain the pasta and toss through with the sauce and basil. Pile high into bowls and top with a chicken breast and a liberal scattering of Parmesan shavings.

OLD-FASHIONED MEATLOAF WITH SWEET MARINARA SAUCE

FOR THE MEATLOAF

1 medium onion, quartered

2 garlic cloves, peeled

a small bunch of fresh thyme, leaves picked

a small bunch of fresh flat-leaf parsley

1 tablespoon dried sage

500g pork mince

500g veal mince

1 tablespoon Worcestershire sauce

1 tablespoon tomato purée

2 eggs, lightly beaten

good grating of whole nutmeg

1 tablespoon fennel seeds

salt and freshly ground black pepper, to taste

275g fresh white breadcrumbs (I like to use sourdough for great flavour and a nice chew)

FOR THE MARINARA SAUCE

400g can cherry tomatoes

200ml passata

1½ teaspoons caster sugar

¼ teaspoon smoked sweet paprika

salt and freshly ground black pepper, to taste

a small handful of fresh basil, torn

SERVES 8

My mum made meatloaf a lot growing up and I have fond memories of how it sat on the plate. There was something about how it seemed so at home, perched next to the mashed potatoes and the winter greens that was a source of comfort. It's one of those things that should never change all that much — which is why this is good and old-fashioned. The classics, sometimes, should remain just that.

To eat this diner-style, take a slice and fry it over a high heat in a little olive oil. Serve on its own or topped with a sunny-side-up fried egg in a sandwich.

---

❶ Preheat the oven to 200ºC/gas mark 6. Line a roasting tray with foil. Start by making the meatloaf. In a food processor, blitz the onion, garlic, thyme and parsley until very fine. Scrape into a large mixing bowl.

❷ Add the sage, pork mince, veal mince, Worcestershire sauce, tomato purée, eggs, nutmeg, fennel seeds, seasoning and breadcrumbs. Using your hands, mix together really well.

❸ Tumble the meatloaf mixture into the prepared roasting tray. Shape the mixture into a rectangular loaf shape about 21 x 13cm. Bake for 15 minutes.

❹ For the marinara sauce, put the cherry tomatoes, passata, sugar, paprika, salt and black pepper in a small saucepan and bring to the boil, allowing the sauce to reduce by a quarter. Remove the meatloaf from the oven and pour the sauce over the top. Add the fresh basil, reduce the oven temperature to 190°C/gas mark 5 and bake the loaf for a further 1¼–1½ hours. To check the loaf is done, insert a meat probe into the centre and look for a reading of 72°C or higher. Or, cut into the centre carefully and peek to make sure there are no pink bits left.

❺ Cut the loaf into 2cm-thick slices. Serve with the marinara sauce, piles of fluffy mashed potatoes and, preferably, collard greens.

SOUTHERN FRIED CHICKEN AND WAFFLES

FOR THE CHICKEN AND WAFFLES
----

1 quantity of Buttermilk fried
    chicken (page 93)
1 quantity of Old-fashioned
    waffles (page 20)
maple syrup, to serve

SERVES 4

The first thing I need to say about chicken and waffles is that
my dad is a very particular eater. He has very specific likes
and dislikes and incredibly high standards and he loves this,
which I think is pretty strong proof that you will too.

Fans of American literature (or Kate Winslet, in that case)
may have heard of *Mildred Pierce*. There are countless reasons
why you should read this book — iconic lead character, insight
into Depression-era America, amazing storyline, yadda, yadda,
yadda — but by far the best part is the food. Mildred goes
into business selling chicken and waffles and, trust me, it's
hard to get through Chapter 6 without brushing the drool away
from the pages.

----

❶ Cook the chicken as per the recipe and keep warm in a low
   oven while you iron the waffles, according to their recipe.

❷ Once you have both elements, simply pile the chicken high
   and baptise in a gleaming stream of golden maple syrup.
   Pure heaven.

SAN FRANCISCO SPAGHETTI WITH CLAMS

FOR THE SPAGHETTI

pinch of salt

350g dried spaghetti

800g fresh palourde clams

2 banana shallots, finely sliced

2 garlic cloves, crushed

50ml extra virgin olive oil

120ml dry white wine

80ml water from the pasta pot

juice and zest of 1 lemon

a large handful of fresh
  flat-leaf parsley,
  roughly chopped

SERVES 4

Pasta is something I crave more than any other food in the world. As well as burgers. And cheese. And often, fried chicken. But it is way up that list. It's stiff competition.

Whenever I'm in the mood for carbs and wine – so every other evening or so – I like to take a trip down by the bay with this recipe. In San Francisco a few years ago, I ordered what I thought would look a little like spaghetti alle vongole with maybe two pin-sized clams. These. Were. Mammoth. They looked like the Jurassic ancestors of clams, so juicy and sweet, bathing in garlic and white wine. But the best thing about this dish is that it takes approximately 15 minutes to make. Enough time to throw on some pyjamas and pretend you're looking out over the Golden Gate Bridge.

❶ Bring a large pan of well-salted water to the boil. Add the spaghetti and cook according to packet instructions until al dente. Pick over the clams and discard any that aren't fully closed or that have a cracked shell.

❷ In a large high-sided frying pan, sauté the shallots and garlic in the oil over a low heat until softened and translucent.

❸ Pour over the wine and reduce by one-third in order to get rid of the raw alcohol flavour. Pour in the pasta water, adding the lemon juice along with it.

❹ In a separate saucepan, cook the clams with a splash of water over a high heat with the lid on. Give the pan an occasional shimmy to make sure the clams are all opening up. This can take up to 5 minutes, so don't panic if they are not all popping open right at once.

❺ Once cooked, strain the clams through a sieve lined with a J Cloth over a bowl to remove any grit, but keep the clean clam juice. Add a splash of this to the wine pan.

❻ Discard any clams that haven't fully opened up and add the good clams to the lemony-wine pan. Throw the drained spaghetti in too and remove from the heat, giving everything a good mix together.

❼ Stir through the parsley and lemon zest, and enjoy.

TIP: If you can't get hold of clams, try this recipe with mussels. It works just as well and the method is exactly the same. Prawns also work well too. Sauté them in the pan with the garlic and shallots with the lid off instead. Seafood heaven.

LOBSTER ROLLS

FOR THE LOBSTER ROLLS

1 x 750–900g live lobster
a small handful of fresh
  flat-leaf parsley, finely
  chopped
juice of ½ lemon
2 tablespoons good-quality
  mayonnaise
salt and freshly ground black
  pepper, to taste
4 small brioche rolls
30g salted butter, melted

SERVES 4

Lobsters in New England are like hot dogs everywhere else –
hot, cheap(ish) and on every street corner. They are native
to the cool New England waters and were so plentiful back in
the early days of Western settlers that they were used as bait
to catch cod and other fish.

The lobster roll is wonderfully down to earth. You have one
of the most prized and valued ingredients in the world served
in a hot-dog bun with fries. In a way, it sums up what so much
of American food is about. Incredible produce, unpretentious
dishes, absolute culinary perfection.

❶ Bring a large pan of water to the boil big enough to hold
the lobster fully submerged.

❷ Place the lobster in the freezer for a minimum of 20 minutes
to ensure that it is fully asleep. Then plunge it straight
into the boiling water and cook until the shell turns bright
red and the small, walking legs can be tugged off easily.
(I find that for every 450g of lobster, it takes about
10 minutes of boiling.)

❸ When the lobster is cooked, remove it from the water and
leave to cool a little. Then remove the meat by cutting the
lobster in half through the head and tail and picking out
the white meat. Crack the claws and pick out this meat too.

❹ Preheat the oven to 180°C/gas mark 4. Chop through the
lobster meat and place it in a mixing bowl with the parsley,
lemon juice, mayo, salt and black pepper. Mix together
gently and check the seasoning.

❺ Slice the brioche rolls three-quarters of the way through,
directly through the top and warm lightly in the oven for
2–3 minutes. Then brush the cut inside with the melted
butter and pile up with the lobster mix. Best enjoyed right
away, with a pile of hot French fries and an ice-cold beer.

NEW ENGLAND
CLAM CHOWDER

FOR THE CLAM CHOWDER

50g salted butter

1 tablespoon olive oil

1 medium onion, finely diced

1 fennel bulb, finely diced

3 rashers unsmoked streaky
  bacon, cut into small pieces

2 garlic cloves, crushed

900g–1kg fresh clams,
  preferably palourde

225g floury potatoes, peeled
  and diced into 1cm cubes

2 sprigs of fresh rosemary,
  leaves finely chopped

500ml milk

220ml double cream

good grating of whole nutmeg

salt and white pepper, to taste

SERVES 4-6

For the record — and so I avoid being subpoenaed by the state of Massachusetts — this is a recipe *based* on a typical New England clam chowder, but with a little personal jujjing up. The core of a New England chowder is a soup made with cream, potatoes, clams and bacon but NO tomatoes. If you even thought about throwing in a handful in there, you would be violating a 1939 Maine bill banning this entirely. If you were after toms, you would be looking at a Manhattan chowder, with a bright red broth and thinner consistency.

❶ Melt the butter and oil together in a large saucepan. Add the onion and fennel and sweat over a low heat for about 8 minutes until really soft and translucent. Throw in the bacon and garlic and cook for a further 5 minutes until everything is starting to smell tantalising.

❷ Pick over the clams, discarding any that aren't fully closed or have cracked shells.

❸ In a separate saucepan, place the good clams and a splash of cold water. Cover and cook over a high heat for 4–6 minutes, shaking occasionally until all the clams have opened.

❹ Drain the clams into a bowl, through a sieve lined with a J Cloth, reserving the clam juice. However, you do *not* want any grit or sand in the final, glorious chowder.

❺ Leave the clams to cool until you can handle them, then pick out the meat from the shells. Reserve a few picturesque ones to use for final serving.

❻ Next, toss the potatoes and rosemary into the onion–fennel pan and stir well. Pour in the milk and cream, seasoning with nutmeg, salt and white pepper to taste. Bring the soup to the boil, then reduce to a simmer for about 10 minutes, stirring occasionally until the potatoes are tender and the whole thing has thickened slightly.

❼ Add the picked clams into the soup, warm through and serve. Pop a couple of the clams in their shells on the top and dive in, with a large hunk of sourdough bread to hand.

BOSTON BAKED BEANS

FOR THE BEANS

500g dried haricot beans,
  soaked overnight in cold
  water and drained
1 medium onion, diced
125g smoked bacon lardons
50g soft dark brown sugar
1 tablespoon cloves
2 tablespoons Dijon mustard
2 heaped tablespoons
  blackstrap molasses
salt and freshly ground
  black pepper, to taste

SERVES 6 (AS A SIDE)

The thing that makes these beans about as typical to Boston as Harvard, *Cheers* and freezing-cold winters, is molasses. During the transatlantic slave trade Boston became an important port and trade spot – especially when it came to rum. Molasses are a by-product of rum production and so the city soon had to find ways to use up its increasingly high amounts of this delicious nectar.

Boston beans are often slow cooked – even overnight if you can resist the insanely delicious aromas wafting from your oven. Puritans who settled in Boston in the seventeenth century could not, by their religious restrictions, labour on the Sabbath, so would throw their baked beans together the night before and slow cook them to eat the next day. Those Puritans were really on to something because if you let these beans take their time, soaking up all that spicy, exotic, treacly flavour, the result is far removed from anything you would normally think of as a baked bean.

❶ Preheat the oven to 130°C/gas mark 1. Put the beans and onion into a large flameproof casserole. Cover with 800ml cold water and bring to the boil, cooking for 10 minutes.

❷ In a frying pan, render the lardons until most of their fat has melted off and they are just starting to turn golden brown and crispy.

❸ Remove the bean pot from the heat and scrape in the bacon, getting all the fat in there too. Add the sugar, cloves, mustard, molasses, salt and black pepper, giving everything a really good mix.

❹ Cover the pot with foil and a tight-fitting lid. Bake for at least 6 hours, or even overnight. Thirty minutes before you want to eat the beans, remove them from the oven, taking off the lid and foil. Boil over a high heat to reduce some of the excess liquid and dive in.

BEST EVER
MAC 'N' CHEESE

FOR THE MAC 'N' CHEESE

- -

40g salted butter

1 garlic clove, crushed

40g plain flour

600ml milk

120g raclette cheese,
  coarsely grated

200g Gruyère cheese,
  coarsely grated

100g strong Cheddar cheese,
  coarsely grated

good grating of whole nutmeg

pinch of white pepper

salt, to taste

pinch of mustard powder

500g dried macaroni pasta

SERVES 8

- -

What is there to say about mac 'n' cheese that hasn't already been put into a ballad, poem or just all-out declaration of love? It's. The. Bomb. There are two kinds of people in the world I don't trust: 1) Those who put their socks on before their underwear; 2) Those who don't like mac 'n' cheese.

This recipe is an amalgamation of ones I've had over the years. So, my disclaimer is that *this* is the recipe I'm using at time of publication. By the time we are hitting Christmas, I might well be using four different types of cheese and going crazy with croûtons. Who knows?!

- -

❶ Bring a large saucepan of salted water to the boil. Meanwhile, in a separate large saucepan, melt the butter and add the garlic, cooking out for 1 minute. Toss in the flour and cook for another minute, stirring constantly.

❷ Remove the pan from the heat and add the milk, a splash at a time, whisking continuously. Continue until all the milk has been poured in. Return the pan to the heat and bring to the boil, stirring continuously, then reduce to a simmer until you have a lovely, smooth, double-cream consistency sauce.

❸ Preheat the grill. Add all three cheeses to the white sauce, stirring until they have fully melted. Season with nutmeg, white pepper, salt and mustard powder. Set aside.

❹ Cook the pasta in the salted, boiling water until al dente, drain and stir through the sauce. Tumble into a shallow dish and pop under the grill to colour the top. Dive in immediately.

FRY BREAD WITH FIXIN'S

FOR THE BREAD

360g plain flour, plus extra
    for dusting
1 tablespoon baking powder
½ teaspoon salt, plus extra
    to serve
240ml warm water
2.5 litres peanut or vegetable
    oil, for frying, plus extra
    for greasing

FOR THE FIXIN'S
----

4 plum tomatoes, diced
a small handful of fresh
    coriander, roughly chopped
60ml soured cream
100g sharp Cheddar cheese,
    coarsely grated
juice of 2 limes

SERVES 6

Fry bread *is* a traditional Native-American food and it
is mighty fine. It is a bread but not in the typical sense.
There's kneading and rising, but you shape it into discs,
rip a hole in the middle and fry it. It's really more of a
doughnut/taco/naan thing but piled high with all the toppings
you could wish for. It's best eaten hot from the fryer but you
can make a batch and then flash them back through a hot oven
up to three days later to bring them back to life. Even better
if you do this when they are rubbed with a little garlic.

----

❶ To make the bread, mix together the flour, baking powder
and salt in a large bowl. Add the warm water and stir using
a cutlery knife before turning out onto a floured surface
and lightly kneading until just coming together. Don't be
worried if the dough is quite wet — it's meant to be a very
soft dough.

❷ Place the dough into a clean, lightly oiled bowl, cover with
clingfilm and leave to rest in a warm place for 1–1½ hours.

❸ Once rested, pour the oil into a large saucepan and heat
gently. To check if it is hot enough, tear off a small piece
of dough and drop it in the oil. If it sizzles, turning
light brown after 30 seconds, you are good to go.

❹ Tear off balls of dough about the size of a ping-pong ball.
Flatten into thin discs using the palms of your hands and
tear a small hole in the centre. Lower carefully into the
hot oil and cook for 1–2 minutes until golden and puffy.
Drain on kitchen paper and sprinkle lightly with salt.
Continue to cook the bread in batches.

❺ Serve the bread on a large platter piled high with all
the fixin's on the table, for people to help themselves.

CAJUN
CREOLE

& SOUTHERN DELICACIES

If there is one type of cooking that totally sums up everything that is great, fascinating, deeply connected and important about American cooking, Creole, Cajun and Southern food would be it. There is no cuisine in the world that offers a bolder example of how food is a living connection to history and culture. The food of the South, of Louisiana, Florida, Georgia, the Carolinas and more, is food that will never leave you feeling unsatisfied or hungry. The first thing you are asked when you walk into a Southern house is 'Y'all hungry?' so you've got no way out of eating until you can barely move. Food comas, mandatory.

When we talk about Cajun cooking, most people think of a general mishmash of rice, shrimp, spice and fried chicken, but it has so much more depth. Firstly, Cajun is different and distinct from Creole — although, these days, they cross over massively. Cajun refers not just to a food style but a group of people called the Acadians who were French settlers in Canada. Expelled from there by the British, they travelled down the Mississippi river to Louisiana and settled mostly in a chunk of land that came to be called Acadiana. It's in the west side of the state, not in New Orleans as a lot of people think. As languages change and people become lazier, their name slurred to Cajun and their food shifted to take advantage of what ingredients were around. The most important part of Cajun cooking, its heart and soul, is the Holy Trinity of ingredients. Onions, green bell peppers and celery are diced up and build the foundation of almost any true Cajun dish. Cajun food is like the second cousin of traditional French cooking, who went travelling and never came back. It uses the same techniques, the Holy Trinity in France would be the *mirepoix*, including carrot, celery and onion, but twists it a little to make it a dish truly of Louisiana.

Creole, on the other hand, is a whole mix of French, Spanish, Native American, Italian and German flavours. It is mostly centred on New Orleans — which, as a port city, got hold of spices, molasses, rice and meats far more frequently than rural parts. It also took to these new ingredients like a duck to water and fully adopted them into Bayou life. Take jambalaya. This is a paella, for all intents and purposes, which no doubt was brought to the table by Spanish settlers and sailors. But add some crayfish and some Creole seasoning and you have something about as synonymous to NOLA as Mardi Gras and Bourbon Street. This isn't a version of paella. This is our jambalaya, baby.

As I said earlier, in this day and age, the distinction is less so. And the food is divine whichever camp it comes from, so don't feel intimidated by the separation. It's just useful to know it exists and where those historical influences came from. And as for Southern food? Well, I'll leave you the recipes for Buttermilk fried chicken (page 93) and Spiced sweet potato pie (page 109) and let you judge for yourselves. Maya Angelou said a lot of smart things but by far her smartest was that 'The best comfort food will always be greens, cornbread and fried chicken'. There is no food in the universe that is more like eating a hug and a blanket from an old friend than Southern cooking. So, welcome home. We've missed you. Y'all hungry?

BUTTERMILK
FRIED CHICKEN

FOR THE CHICKEN

600g boneless, skinless
  chicken thighs
600ml buttermilk
1½ teaspoons clear honey
1 tablespoon salt
2 litres peanut oil or
  vegetable oil, for frying
250g plain flour
75g cornflour
2 teaspoons garlic powder
1 tablespoon Cajun seasoning
freshly ground black pepper,
  to taste

SERVES 4

I had some fried chicken in Memphis that changed my life. Gus's World Famous Fried Chicken was the sacred place – and while I'm not sure how much of the world they are known in, I've certainly yammered on about them enough that they might be a little closer to that goal now.

I asked how exactly they managed to get their chicken so crisp but still so juicy, so crunchy, but still so clean tasting… all at the same time!? Needless to say, the waitress wouldn't tell me the secrets but she did say that they fry their birds in peanut oil. I've heard this a few times, so if you can get your hands on some it might just be your golden ticket to fried chicken perfection.

---

❶ Trim any excess fat, sinew or fragments of bone off the chicken thighs. Put them in a large Tupperware container with the buttermilk, honey and salt. Mix well and leave to marinate in the fridge overnight.

❷ The next day, heat the oil gently in a large saucepan. Put the plain flour, cornflour, garlic powder, Cajun seasoning and black pepper in a wide, shallow dish and combine well.

❸ Check the oil is hot enough by popping in a small chunk of bread. If it sizzles and goes brown within 30 seconds, you're good to go. Preheat the oven to 200°C/gas mark 6. Shake any excess marinade off the thighs, then dunk them into the flour mix. Cover the thighs well.

❹ Pinch the thighs on one end with long tongs and carefully lower them into the oil, making sure to swirl them around a little – still holding one end out of the oil – before gently plopping the whole thing in. Cook in batches for 2-3 minutes until golden and crispy on the outside, then drain on some kitchen paper.

❺ Finish the thighs off on a baking tray in the oven, cooking them for an additional 6-8 minutes while you fry, then oven-cook the remainder in batches.

MUSSEL AND CHORIZO JAMBALAYA

FOR THE JAMBALAYA

----

1 tablespoon vegetable oil

100g cooking chorizo, sliced into rings

1 large onion, finely diced

2 sticks celery, finely diced

1 green pepper, core and seeds removed, finely diced

2 garlic cloves, crushed

2 teaspoons Cajun seasoning

250g long-grain rice

1 tablespoon tomato purée

350ml hot chicken stock

500g live mussels

salt and freshly ground black pepper, to taste

a small handful of fresh flat-leaf parsley, roughly chopped

lemon wedges, to serve (optional)

SERVES 4

It's hard to pick one US city that singularly sums up the idea of a 'melting pot' but New Orleans is a pretty strong candidate. You only have to walk the streets to notice how the French, Spanish, Germans and British all left their mark on the architecture, music and most importantly, food.

Jambalaya is a Creole dish, with its origins in Spanish paella. Everything about it makes it the epitome of Louisiana Creole cuisine. Firstly, it uses the Holy Trinity of celery, onions and bell peppers as well as being cooked all together in one pot — another cornerstone of this type of cooking. Secondly, it is constantly developing and changing, taking on new traditions and characteristics with everyone who claims it as their own.

----

❶ Heat the oil in a large, wide frying pan and sauté the chorizo for a minute. Add the onion, celery and green pepper, sweating for about 5 minutes until nice and soft.

❷ Add the garlic before tossing in the Cajun seasoning and stir well. Pour in the rice and tomato purée followed by the chicken stock. Cover the pan with a tight-fitting lid and simmer for 6 minutes.

❸ Remove the lid and place the mussels around the pan, giving them each enough space. Cover with the lid and continue to cook for a further 6 minutes. Remove from the heat and set aside for 5 minutes to steam the rice. Then taste the rice — it should be al dente and the mussels wide open. Make sure to throw away any that have not opened their shells. Stir through some salt and black pepper and the parsley.

❹ Serve with lemon wedges if you like, and imagine that you are sitting on the dock of the bayou.

BUTTER-BAKED CAJUN PRAWNS

FOR THE PRAWNS

16 raw king prawns, deveined
   and shells removed but heads
   and tails left on
¼ teaspoon Worcestershire sauce
juice of ½ lemon
few drops of Tabasco
2 teaspoons Cajun seasoning
100g salted butter, melted
1 garlic clove, crushed
salt and freshly ground black
   pepper, to taste
2 spring onions, sliced thinly
   on the diagonal

SERVES 2

Everything is better with butter. Julia Child was definitely onto something.

Sometimes it's best to keep things simple and this recipe supports that. A touch of spice, a few prawns, a wodge of butter... what could go wrong? I completely strip my prawns, mostly so that I can just plunge in the second this bad boy comes out of the oven, but if you want a bit more of a hands-on dish, then by all means keep these whole and do the undressing once cooked.

----

❶ Preheat the oven to 200°C/gas mark 6. Line a small, shallow roasting tray with foil and add the prawns. Set aside.

❷ In a small bowl or jug, mix together the Worcestershire sauce, lemon juice, Tabasco, Cajun seasoning, melted butter, garlic, salt and black pepper. Pour over the prawns and cook for 8–10 minutes.

❸ Remove from the oven and sprinkle with spring onions. Best enjoyed with fresh, crusty bread nearby to soak up all the spicy, buttery goodness.

NOLA CHICKEN AND SAUSAGE GUMBO

FOR THE GUMBO

40g salted butter

2 tablespoons olive oil

1 large white onion, finely
  diced

3 sticks celery, finely diced

1 green pepper, core and seeds
  removed, finely diced

3 garlic cloves, crushed

1½ teaspoons dried oregano

1½ teaspoons dried thyme

1 teaspoon cayenne pepper

½ teaspoon ground mace

1 teaspoon smoked sweet paprika

few drops of Tabasco

40g plain flour

1 litre hot chicken stock

500g boneless and skinless
  chicken thighs

1 tablespoon vegetable oil

200g smoked sausage, sliced

150g fresh okra, sliced in half
  on the diagonal (optional)

salt and freshly ground black
  pepper, to taste

SERVES 6

Gumbo IS Creole food. This simple soup is the absolute, purest
example of what American food is all about. Its name comes
from the Bantu word for 'okra'. Its technique is that of
a French *bouillabaisse* thickened with a roux. Its spices
come from the port history of New Orleans, where different
ingredients and flavourings were circulating. And the Choctaw
use *filé* powder – a kind of seasoning – to flavour it. AND it's
cooked in one big melting pot. This IS American food.

This gumbo can take any meats or shellfish you want to throw
in there. My one non-negotiable is that it must have smoked
sausage. In Louisiana it would be andouille (a smoked pork
sausage) but any smoked sausage will do.

----

❶ Melt the butter and olive oil in a large saucepan. Add the
onion, celery and green pepper, sweating for about 5 minutes
until nice and soft. Toss in the garlic and cook for a
further minute.

❷ Tip the oregano, thyme, cayenne, mace, paprika and Tabasco
into the pot, giving everything a good stir. Add the flour
and cook out, whisking constantly for 1 minute. Remove from
the heat and pour in the stock a splash at a time, mixing
until there are no lumps.

❸ Return the pan to the heat, bring to the boil, then reduce
the heat to a simmer. You want the soup to thicken just
a touch.

❹ Cut the chicken thighs into bite-sized pieces and then sear
off in a separate frying pan in half the vegetable oil. You
want to get a good colour on them. Add these to the gumbo.

❺ Repeat with the sausage, making sure to get some good colour
on the meat before adding to the pot.

❻ Simmer the gumbo for 20–25 minutes until the chicken is
cooked through. If you want to add okra, do this after
10 minutes. Season to taste. Serve over rice or with crusty
French bread on the side.

SHRIMP AND GRITS

FOR THE SHRIMP

50g salted butter

1 garlic clove, crushed

pinch of Cajun seasoning

few drops of Tabasco

salt and freshly ground black
  pepper, to taste

400g raw king prawns, peeled,
  deveined and heads removed
  but tails left on

6 spring onions, sliced

juice of 1 lemon

a small bunch of fresh flat-leaf
  parsley, roughly chopped

FOR THE GRITS

190g grits, or coarse polenta

30g Parmesan cheese, grated

45g salted butter

50ml double cream

salt and freshly ground black
  pepper, to taste

SERVES 4

If you Google, 'What is the difference between grits and
polenta?' you will come across a number of websites and blog
posts that contain more hostility than all of Taylor Swift's
songs about her exes combined.

In a nutshell, grits are made from hominy, a type of corn
native to the US. Traditionally, it was boiled and treated
with wood ash to produce a bright white cornmeal, rather than
a golden yellow one more like polenta. But perhaps the most
important difference is that this one is found in the South;
the area stretching from Louisiana to North and South Carolina
is called The Grits Belt.

Grits can be tricky to get your hands on, so feel free to
substitute polenta instead. Just keep it to yourself if you're
ever in Charleston.

❶ Start by making the grits. Bring 1 litre of salted water
  to the boil in a large saucepan. Tip in the grits, stirring
  as you pour. Bring to the boil, then reduce to a simmer,
  leaving to bubble for 13–15 minutes. Whisk regularly.

❷ Once the grits look like a thick, oozing porridge, remove
  from the heat and stir through the Parmesan, butter and
  cream. Check the seasoning, then set aside.

❸ For the shrimp, melt the butter in a frying pan and sauté
  the garlic for 1 minute. Tip in the Cajun seasoning,
  Tabasco, salt and black pepper, stirring well.

❹ Add the prawns to the pan and fry for 2–3 minutes until
  bright pink and opaque white all the way through. Add the
  spring onions and finish with the lemon juice. Remove from
  the heat and stir through the parsley.

❺ Ladle the grits into pasta bowls and top with a spoonful
  of shrimp and a generous glug of sauce.

DEEP-FRIED OYSTERS WITH HERBY DRESSING

FOR THE OYSTERS

12 live oysters
1 litre vegetable oil,
   for frying 85g plain flour
½ teaspoon salt
½ teaspoon bicarbonate of soda
3 tablespoons cornflour, plus
   extra for dusting
200ml cold sparkling water

FOR THE DRESSING

50ml extra virgin olive oil
1 teaspoon Dijon mustard
juice and zest of 1 lemon
a very small handful of fresh
   dill, finely chopped
a very small handful of fresh
   basil, finely chopped
a very small handful of fresh
   flat-leaf parsley, finely
   chopped
30g capers, drained, rinsed
   and roughly chopped
3 tablespoons white wine
   vinegar
½ tablespoon runny honey
salt and freshly ground black
   pepper, to taste

SERVES 2 (AS A LIGHT(ISH) LUNCH)

The writer Jonathan Swift once said, 'He was a bold man that first ate an oyster' and damn, was he right. If someone looked at you, dead in the eye, holding up what looks like, essentially, a rock, then asked you to force it open with a knife, scoop out the salty, sloppy flesh from inside and shoot it like a tequila slammer, are you honestly telling me you wouldn't question their sanity? I would.

This batter is essentially a tempura batter – very light and loose that crisps up incredibly in the hot oil. You only need to colour the batter, not cook the oysters through otherwise they'll go tough and chewy rather than tender and yielding. So let them take a quick dip in the fryer, fishing them out swiftly and gobbling down with abandon.

----

❶ Place the oysters curved-side down on a chopping board. Find the hinge of the oyster shell and the join between the two shells and force your way into it using the tip of a short, strong knife. Wiggle your knife all the way around the shell to release the two halves and then scrape out the oyster onto a plate. Do this with all the oysters then set aside.

❷ Mix the dressing ingredients together in a small bowl and set aside.

❸ Heat the oil in a large, high-sided saucepan and then make the batter. Mix the flour, salt, bicarbonate of soda and cornflour together in a medium bowl. Gradually add the sparkling water, whisking as you go. The batter will look quite thin.

❹ Dredge the oysters in a little cornflour and then dunk them into the batter to coat. To test if the oil is hot enough, drip in a little batter from the end of a teaspoon. If it sizzles and turns golden within 20 seconds, you are good to go. Using tongs, lower the oysters into the hot oil and cook for about 30 seconds each or until the batter is golden and crisp. Fry the oysters in 2-3 batches, depending on the size of the pan. Leave to drain on kitchen paper and sprinkle with a little salt.

❺ Serve the oysters immediately with the dressing and, ideally, a margarita.

BLACKENED CAJUN SNAPPER

FOR THE SNAPPER

2 teaspoons dried thyme

2 teaspoons dried marjoram

2 teaspoons onion powder

2 teaspoons garlic powder

2 teaspoons smoked sweet
   paprika

1 teaspoon cayenne pepper

salt and freshly ground
   black pepper, to taste

30g salted butter

1 tablespoon olive oil

2 red snapper fillets,
   skin on, pin-boned

SERVES 2

Dishes that are blackened and burnt are some of my favourite food. They feature a lot in this book, which I think says a great deal about my concentration span. If it can take a little scorching, I'm game.

Blackening fish is a common Southern way of cooking, especially in Florida and Louisiana – anywhere that fish is readily available. The spice rub and searingly hot butter join forces to form a charcoal-picante crust around the fish. Don't be afraid to give it some colour. For once you can say 'It's meant to be black' with conviction.

❶ Mix the dried herbs, onion and garlic powders, spices and seasoning together on a plate. Heat the butter and oil in a wide frying pan until very, VERY hot.

❷ Dip the fish fillets in the spice rub, coating them really well on both sides. Then lower the fish, skin-side first, into the frying pan. The pan will start to smoke but don't worry – for once you want it black! Cook the fish for 3 minutes per side, depending on the thickness of your fillets.

❸ Remove the fish from the pan and leave to rest for 5 minutes. Delicious served with BBQ spring onions with rosemary and hazelnut butter (page 64), potato salad and a cold beer.

CHEDDAR AND CARAWAY SEED HUSHPUPPIES

FOR THE HUSHPUPPIES

130g mature Cheddar cheese,
  coarsely grated
150g self-raising flour
275g fine cornmeal
1 tablespoon caraway seeds
pinch of mustard powder
150ml milk
300ml buttermilk
salt and freshly ground
  black pepper, to taste
1 litre vegetable oil,
  for frying

MAKES 40-50 HUSHPUPPIES

I first came across this unlikely flavour combination in a Yotam Ottolenghi recipe. It works so well in almost any baked goods — from scones to savoury shortbread to just plain old bread.

These are the perfect bar snack and super quick to make. The story goes that soldiers during the Civil War would toss little balls of fried cornbread to their dogs to shut them up in case the enemy heard them — to hush their puppies. But today they're more common on a bar bench, next to some hot sauce and a cold Coors Light.

----

❶ Mix together the Cheddar, flour, cornmeal, caraway seeds and mustard powder in a large mixing bowl. Add the milk, buttermilk, salt and black pepper, and stir until you have a thick batter.

❷ Heat the oil in a high-sided saucepan and check to see if it's ready by spooning in a small amount of the batter. It should sizzle and turn golden within about 30 seconds.

❸ Using two teaspoons, scrape off little chunks of dough into the oil, fishing them out after about 30 seconds once golden and puffy, and set aside to drain on kitchen paper. These are delicious dunked in Foolproof guacamole (page 131) and salsa.

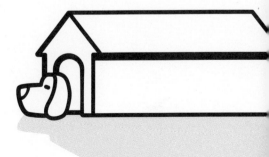

CRAB CAKE PO' BOY WITH LIME SOURED CREAM

FOR THE CRAB CAKES

250g white crabmeat
2 spring onions
1 green pepper, core and
    seeds removed
80g panko breadcrumbs
¾ teaspoon garlic powder
few drops of Tabasco
1 egg
salt and freshly ground
    black pepper, to taste
450ml vegetable oil,
    for frying

FOR THE SANDWICH

300ml soured cream
zest of 2 limes
4 submarine rolls
1 beefsteak tomato, sliced
2 Little Gem lettuces, shredded
½ cucumber, sliced

SERVES 4-6

Like so many American dishes, a po' boy in and of itself
is nothing remarkable. It's just a sandwich, really. But done
right, with the perfect fillings and a good level of respect
for its origins, it's something special.

Back when New Orleans was a real hub of shipping activity,
dockhands and labourers headed into the city to get something
to eat. But many didn't have enough money to even look at most
restaurant menus, so they would go up to the kitchen doors and
ask for any scraps of food to be made into a little sandwich.
They were literally 'poor boys' and so this life-saving
sandwich got its name.

The best po' boys I've had have *always* had some kind of fried
seafood filling, heaps of salad and a swooshing of sauce.

❶ To make the crab cakes, put the crabmeat in a large mixing
   bowl and remove any fragments of shell.

❷ Blitz the spring onions and green pepper together in a
   food processor to a slightly coarse mush and add to the
   crab. Blitz the breadcrumbs in the food processor and tip
   into the mix. Add the garlic powder, Tabasco, egg, salt and
   black pepper and combine well.

❸ Heat the oil in a wide, high-sided frying pan. When hot,
   take tablespoon-sized amounts of the crab-cake mix and roll
   gently to form discs about 2.5cm thick. Fry on each side for
   1 minute until golden brown, then drain on kitchen paper.
   Cook in 2-3 batches depending on the size of the pan.

❹ To make the lime soured cream, mix together the soured
   cream, lime zest, salt and black pepper in a small bowl.
   Set aside.

❺ Split the submarine rolls in half lengthways and spread
   liberally with the lime soured cream. Build up with the
   tomato, lettuce and cucumber, and place the crab cakes
   on top. Top with the upper crust of the roll and dive in.

CURRIED PEANUT SOUP

FOR THE SOUP

50g salted butter

2 tablespoons olive oil

1 large onion, finely diced

2 sticks celery, finely diced

salt and freshly ground black
  pepper, to taste

2 garlic cloves, crushed

3 tablespoons plain flour

1 tablespoon garam marsala

1 tablespoon ground cumin

1 tablespoon ground coriander

1 teaspoon ground cinnamon

1 teaspoon ground turmeric

1 teaspoon cayenne pepper

1 litre hot chicken stock

340g jar smooth peanut butter

150ml single cream

50g peanuts, roasted and
  roughly chopped, to serve

1 whole red chilli, sliced
  thinly on the diagonal,
  to serve

SERVES 6

If you hadn't noticed, Americans. Love. Peanut. Butter. They spend $800 million a year on the stuff and the nuts themselves are officially America's number-one snack.

I came across this true Southern recipe when reading about dishes synonymous with the state of Virginia. Because peanuts grew so plentifully, and were filling and cheap, peanut soup was often used to feed slaves. Peanuts, then, are incredibly rooted in US history and culture – much more so than it may seem when looking at a jar in an aisle in a supermarket.

❶ In a large saucepan, melt the butter and olive oil until just foaming. Add the onion, celery and a pinch of salt, and cover with a circle of greaseproof paper dampened with water. Put the lid on and sweat well over a low heat for 8–10 minutes until totally soft and translucent.

❷ Remove the damp paper and add the garlic, cooking for about 1 minute. Then add the flour, spices and black pepper and stir constantly, cooking this out for a further 2 minutes.

❸ Remove the pan from the heat and whisk in the chicken stock a little at a time, making sure that there are no floury lumps in the pan before adding in the next splosh. Once all the stock is added, return the pan to the heat and bring to the boil before reducing the heat to a simmer. Leave, uncovered, for about 15 minutes until the mixture has thickened to a single-cream consistency.

❹ Next, melt the peanut butter in a small saucepan until it is a drizzling consistency and then pour into a blender. Add the soup from the pan and blitz until smooth and unctuous.

❺ Strain the soup through a sieve into a clean saucepan and finish off with the cream. Beautiful garnished with some chopped, roasted peanuts and fresh red chilli slices – if you are feeling brave.

TIP: If you want to make this ahead and freeze it, follow the steps until straining it. Do this right into a Tupperware container and when you defrost it, heat through gently, adding the cream before serving.

BISCUITS AND SAUSAGE GRAVY

FOR THE BISCUITS

310g plain flour, plus extra
    for dusting
¼ teaspoon bicarbonate of soda
1 tablespoon baking powder
1 teaspoon salt
90g cold unsalted butter,
    cut into 1cm cubes
240ml buttermilk

FOR THE GRAVY

400g good-quality sausages
    (I like to use Italian
    sausages or Cumberland)
1 tablespoon olive oil
55g plain flour
pinch of cayenne pepper
pinch of mustard powder
690ml milk
salt and freshly ground black
    pepper, to taste

SERVES 6-8 (MAKES 13 BISCUITS)

This dish is unbelievably weird to my British friends and family. The biscuits are a kind of light, savoury scone-bread love-child that are almost emblems of Southern hospitality. They are also great dunked in soup or split in half and filled with crispy bacon or even just buttered and jammed. And the gravy? It's not brown but more of a white sauce, which is delectably moreish.

I have to say, wonderfully weird and way out there as it may sound, everybody who's tried this has booked a one-way flight straight to Tennessee. Like John Lennon meant to say, give biscuits a chance.

❶ Preheat the oven to 190°C/gas mark 5, for the biscuits. Line a baking tray with baking parchment. Mix the flour, bicarbonate of soda, baking powder and salt together in the bowl of a food processor.

❷ Add the butter and blitz for 30 seconds–1 minute until it resembles fine breadcrumbs. Then, with the motor running, add the buttermilk until just combined. Don't overwork it or the biscuits will be tough and not lighter than air.

❸ Turn the dough out onto a lightly floured surface and knead a couple of times, just to bring the dough together. It will feel very soft at this stage. Roll it out gently to about 2cm thick and stamp out circles 7cm in diameter.

❹ Place the biscuits on the prepared baking tray, with space in between for them to expand. Bake for 12–15 minutes until golden and puffed up. Leave to cool on a wire rack.

❺ Then make the gravy. Start by running a knife down the side of the sausages to remove their casings. Then chop the unsheathed meat into chunks and fry gently in a saucepan in the olive oil, smooshing with a wooden spoon to break up the chunks. Once cooked through, sprinkle over the flour, cayenne and mustard powder. Stir through the sausage and cook out for about 2 minutes until lightly browned in colour.

❻ Add the milk a splash at a time, off the heat, making sure there are no lumps. Then return to the heat and cook out, stirring constantly, until thickened — it should be like a white sauce in consistency. Check the seasoning then pour over the biscuits. A true Southern delight.

SPICED SWEET POTATO PIE

FOR THE PASTRY

250g plain flour, plus extra
  for dusting
140g cold salted butter,
  cut into 1cm cubes
pinch of salt
2 egg yolks

FOR THE FILLING

2 large sweet potatoes
110g salted butter, cut into
  1cm cubes
2 eggs
1 teaspoon ground mixed spice
1 teaspoon ground ginger
½ teaspoon ground nutmeg
2 teaspoons vanilla extract
zest of 1 orange
icing sugar, for dusting
  (optional)
whipped cream, to serve

SERVES 6-8 DEPENDING ON THICKNESS OF SLICE

It's a pretty solid rule that if Ray Charles has written
a song about something, you can be sure that it is pretty
special. This is definitely the case with spiced sweet potato
pie. As Ray puts it, this Southern baked treat is softer than
a lullaby and soulful as a baby's cry.

This is a firm holiday favourite, mostly because it's pretty
idiot-proof, so if you are battling the lasting effects of
last night's rum punch, you're in with a fighting chance. The
tricky thing is patience. You've got to cook the filling until
it's just set, all while the tantalising aromas are drifting
from your kitchen, through your home and into your heart.

❶ To make the pastry, put the flour, butter and salt together
in a food processor and blitz until it resembles fine
breadcrumbs. Tip into a bowl. Mix in the egg yolks and
4 tablespoons of cold water then bring the pastry together
with your hands, taking care not to handle it too much.

❷ Turn the pastry out onto a floured surface and roll to
3mm thick. Line a 24cm deep fluted pie tin with the pastry,
leaving any excess to hang over the edge. Chill for at least
30 minutes until firm. Preheat the oven to 190°C/gas mark 5.

❸ Meanwhile, make the filling. Stab the sweet potatoes and cook
in the microwave for 12 minutes at 800W until softened. Cut
in half lengthways and leave to cool a little before using
a spoon to scoop out their flesh into a freestanding mixer
bowl. (Or simply bake the potatoes whole, in the 190°C/gas
mark 5 oven for an hour or until soft in the middle.)

❹ Line the chilled pastry with greaseproof paper and weight
with baking beans before baking for 20 minutes.

❺ Check the sides of the pastry are dry and sandy before
removing the paper and beans and baking for a further
7 minutes to cook through. Reduce the oven temperature
to 180°C/gas mark 4.

❻ Beat the potato to cool it before adding the butter. Once
incorporated, add the eggs, one at a time, before adding
the mixed spice, ginger, nutmeg, vanilla and orange zest.
Pour the filling into the pie case and bake for 1 hour-1 hour
10 minutes until the filling is set. Leave to cool on a wire
rack before dusting with icing sugar, if you like, and
enjoying with dizzying amounts of whipped cream.

NEW ORLEANS BEIGNETS WITH CINNAMON SUGAR

FOR THE BEIGNETS

- 55ml warm water
- 7g fast-action dried yeast
- 55g caster sugar
- 240ml milk
- 115ml vegetable oil
- 1 egg, lightly beaten
- 510g plain flour, plus extra for dusting
- pinch of salt
- 1.5 litres vegetable oil, for frying
- 150g icing sugar
- 2 teaspoons ground cinnamon

MAKES 16 BEIGNETS

If you are planning on visiting New Orleans, take note of Colman Andrews' top tip: 'Do not visit Café Du Monde, in the French Quarter of New Orleans, wearing black'. This is not for any voodoo-superstitious-beware-of-the-spirits kind of thing. It's because you will get *covered* in icing sugar and there is no amount of swatting, rubbing or dabbing in the world that will get it out. You will have been marked as a beignet eater for the rest of the day.

Beignet literally translates into English as 'fritter' and they aren't your run-of-the-mill doughnut. They are little square pillows that puff up hugely when dunked in hot oil and are characteristically smothered in icing sugar while still warm from the fryer.

---

❶ Mix the water, yeast, sugar, milk, vegetable oil and egg together in a large mixing bowl. Sift in the flour and salt, and stir well using a cutlery knife. Cover the mixture with a piece of oiled clingfilm and leave to rise in a warm place for 1 hour. The mixture will grow slightly but this is more so it can relax and remain tender when cooked.

❷ Heat the oil for frying in a large, high-sided saucepan. Tip the dough out onto a floured surface and roll into a rough 28cm square, 1cm thick. Using a pizza wheel or knife, cut the square into 16 smaller squares.

❸ Sift the icing sugar and cinnamon onto a lipped tray.

❹ To test if the oil is hot enough, drop in a piece of dough and if it sizzles and turns golden within 25 seconds, you are good to go. Using tongs, carefully lower each beignet, in batches of four, into the hot oil. They will puff up and almost double in size, so don't overcrowd the pan. They are ready when they are a deep golden brown and feel very light for their size. Break one in half to make sure they are not doughy or soggy in the middle.

❺ Remove the beignets from the oil and drain on kitchen paper, then toss in the cinnamon sugar while warm. Enjoy with a strong cup of coffee.

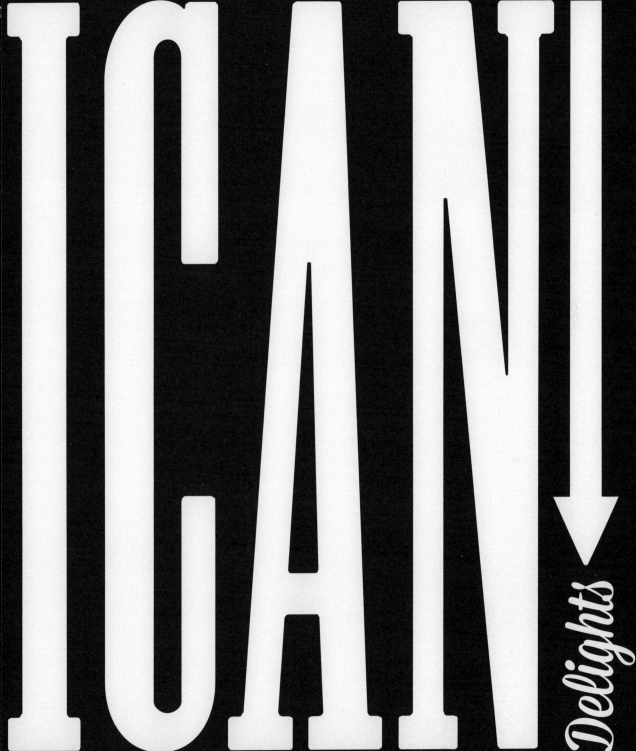

When I was in Chicago a few years ago, I ate a fish taco so divine that it almost made me cry. I remember it vividly, like the way some people remember rampant flings and others crazy, endless nights partying on the beach.

It was lightly floured tilapia, deep-fried and served in a mini soft corn tortilla with a pineapple-jalapeño pico de gallo. It was bliss.

The mothership that bore this Latina lovely was Big Star Taqueria – an outdoor, too cool for words, cheap and cheerful, $3-a-beer place right next to the Damen-O'Hare El stop. You wouldn't be able to find this place unless you did a little bit of clicking on websites or flicking through guidebooks, and I cannot tell you how happy I am that we did just that. It's not exactly tourist town. There are local hipsters and artisanal coffee shops, but this isn't where Frank Lloyd Wright worked or where The Bean sits. When I first met my friend Amy, Chicago-born and raised, I asked her if she had been, to which she said 'Yeah… how have *you* been there?'. So, yep, it was a little schlep to get to from our hostel in Little Greece. But we *flew* back from San Francisco to Chicago, pretty much just to have these tacos before flying home. I would go almost anywhere for good Mexican.

To ignore the Mexican influence in American food would be unforgivable. More than that, it would be downright incorrect. Mexico and the United States have always shared a blurred historical line, with states like Texas and New Mexico being passed to and fro, and divvied up chunk by chunk over many years. So rather than being two separate, unfriendly relatives, I prefer to think of these two culinary wonderlands as familiar cousins, who share more characteristics than they think.

I've said before how that unforgettable chilli flavour is a true building block of American cuisine and it still stands. Can you even begin to imagine not seeing a taco truck, precariously perched on a street corner of LA? Or what would take the place of your burrito at lunchtime? Or not knowing the joy of a melting, oozy, quesadilla, chowed down after a big night out? Mexican food *is* a huge part of American food.

The recipes in this chapter are exactly that – recipes of crossover. I am not pretending to be a pro at Mexican cooking, and no I can't handle any chilli heat over a couple of Scovilles, but these dishes are more a representation of what happens when cultures mix than when they stay pure. And I think there is something beautiful in that.

STEAK TACOS WITH CHILLI AND BITTER CHOCOLATE

FOR THE TACOS

4 mini flour tortillas

50ml vegetable oil

salt and freshly ground black
  pepper, to taste

2 x 175–200g sirloin steaks

2 garlic cloves, crushed

juice of 1 lime

½ tablespoon chipotle paste

sprig of fresh thyme

5 cherry tomatoes, quartered

3 spring onions, cut into thin
  pieces on the diagonal

a small bunch of fresh
  coriander, leaves picked
  and roughly chopped

a small bunch of fresh mint,
  leaves picked and roughly
  chopped

4 tablespoons extra virgin
  olive oil

good grating of 100 per cent
  cocoa solids dark chocolate
  (I like to use Willie's Cacao)

1 red chilli, cut into thin
  slices on the diagonal,
  to serve

soured cream, to serve

wedges of lime, to serve
  (optional)

SERVES 2

I try to sneak chocolate into everything, the same way people try to sneak healthy vegetables into anything that was once delicious and perfect (see Brownies, Raw or Root Veg, Crisps).

This dish is no exception – plus the use of 100 per cent pure cacao here is pretty authentic so, kudos. Chocolate has long been praised and celebrated in Mexican culture, starting with the Aztecs way back when they realised the perks of chocolate right from the get go. Still today, cacao is used very often as a seasoning rather than simply as a way to get through a break-up or a slow weekend. You need the darkest chocolate you can get your hands on and grate it very finely.

❶ Toast the tortillas in a dry frying pan until just browning at the edges. Set aside on a plate.

❷ In the same pan, heat 1 tablespoon of the vegetable oil. Season the steaks generously and pan-fry to rare for 2–2½ minutes per side, depending on thickness. Put the remaining vegetable oil, the garlic, lime juice, chipotle paste and thyme in a bowl and mix to together. Add the steaks and leave to marinate.

❸ Meanwhile, mix together the tomatoes, spring onions, coriander, mint, olive oil and some salt and black pepper, and set aside.

❹ Remove the steaks from the marinade (discard the marinade) and slice into thin strips. Cover with a decent grating of chocolate.

❺ Serve the tortillas with the steaks, salsa, chilli, soured cream and lime wedges, if you like, at the table in separate bowls, allowing everyone to customise their tacos.

CHORIZO AND MINT FLAUTAS

FOR THE FLAUTAS

200g cooking chorizo, diced
1 medium onion, finely diced
2 garlic cloves, crushed
1 red chilli, finely diced
6 Cumberland sausages
a large handful of fresh mint,
   finely chopped
salt and freshly ground black
   pepper, to taste
8 mini flour tortillas
150–175ml vegetable oil,
   for frying

SERVES 4

If you have ever wished that somebody would Frankenstein-up a hard taco, a fajita and a spring roll into one unique culinary delight, then let me introduce you to the flauta.

This is a tortilla, filled with picante, rich, strong spice and cooling, medicinal mint, rolled up real tight and deep-fried.

If you are ever travelling through the South West US, especially Arizona or New Mexico, make sure you try these. Dip liberally into red salsa and have an ice-cold beer nearby to soothe any rogue chilli punches.

❶ Fry the chorizo in a large, high-sided frying pan over a low heat. You want to render off as much fat as possible, leaving a crimson oil in the pan.

❷ Add the onion, garlic and chilli and sauté over a medium heat for about 10 minutes until softened and slightly coloured.

❸ Run a sharp knife down the edge of the sausages, removing them from their casings. Tear the sausage meat into chunks and cook it in the chorizo pan for 3–4 minutes. Squish the sausage to break it down and cook all the way through.

❹ Remove the pan from the heat and leave to cool slightly. Stir through the mint, salt and black pepper. Then, take a tortilla and heap a decent amount of sausage in the middle. Roll up into a long cigar shape and secure through the middle with a cocktail stick.

❺ Repeat until all the sausage mix is safely tucked away inside the tortillas. Then heat the vegetable oil in a heavy-bottomed saucepan. Check the oil is ready to fry by dropping a teeny bit of tortilla into the oil. If it sizzles and dances on the top right away, you're good to go.

❻ Fry the flautas on all sides, turning gently. They only need about 15 seconds on each side so be careful not to burn them. (You will need to cook in 2 batches.) Drain on kitchen paper, remove the cocktail sticks and serve with Foolproof guacamole (page 131).

BAJA FISH TACOS WITH PICO DE GALLO

FOR THE TACOS

- -

1.5 litres sunflower oil,
  for frying

8 mini corn tortillas

3 white fish fillets (any will
  do, pollock is nice and cheap
  but cod works well), skinned
  and pin-boned

100g matzo meal or panko
  breadcrumbs

½ teaspoon smoked hot paprika

2 eggs, lightly beaten

70g plain flour

FOR THE PICO DE GALLO

- -

2 corn on the cob

1 red chilli, plus extra
  to serve

1 small red onion, finely diced

3 plum tomatoes, deseeded
  and diced

a small handful of fresh
  coriander, roughly chopped

juice of 1 lime

2 tablespoons extra virgin
  olive oil

salt and freshly ground black
  pepper, to taste

soured cream, to serve

wedges of lime, to serve

SERVES 4

- -

'Pico de gallo' is one of my all-time favourite food names. It means 'rooster's beak'. Maybe because of the similarity between the way chickens and people peck at it? Who knows.

These tacos originate from the Baja region of Mexico, slap bang on the coast, hence the fish. They have been California-fied in recent years and are a fundamental dish of Tex Mex restaurants up and down the U.S. of A. Crispy, yielding flakes of white fish, bitter, blackened corn and just a hint of a kick from the red chilli.

- -

❶ For the tacos, pour the oil into a heavy-bottomed saucepan, preferably a flameproof casserole, and heat over a medium heat. (If you have a deep-fat fryer, heat to about 180°C.)

❷ Meanwhile, toast the tortillas gently in a dry frying pan on both sides until just charred at the edges. Transfer to a plate and set aside.

❸ For the pico de gallo, shuck the corn by running a knife down the length of each cob to remove the kernels. Place these in the dry frying pan and char, shaking occasionally. Once they are slightly scorched, after about 5 minutes, remove them from the pan and place in a mixing bowl.

❹ Add the chilli to the pan and char all over. Transfer to a chopping board, deseed and finely slice. Add to the corn. Add the onion and tomatoes to the corn bowl. Stir through the coriander with the lime juice and olive oil, and season with salt and black pepper. Mix thoroughly and set aside.

❺ Cut the fish fillets into strips about 2cm wide and 10cm long. In one bowl, mix together the matzo meal and paprika. Put the beaten eggs in another bowl and the flour into a third. Coat the fish, first in the flour, then the beaten eggs and finally the matzo meal until all the strips are covered.

❻ Check the oil is hot enough to fry by dropping a pinch of the matzo crumbs in. If they sizzle and bounce right back up to the top, you are good to go. Fry the fish for 3-4 minutes in batches of about three strips at a time then gently rescue with a slotted spoon and drain on kitchen paper. Serve the tortillas, fish and pico de gallo at the table, with soured cream, wedges of lime and extra sliced chillies for those who want to show off.

ENCHILADAS WITH ROASTED SQUASH, BLACK BEANS AND MARJORAM

FOR THE ENCHILADAS

----

1 large red onion, finely diced

3 carrots, peeled and chopped
  into 1cm cubes

1 butternut squash, peeled,
  deseeded and chopped into
  1cm cubes

2 garlic cloves, crushed

3 tablespoons fresh marjoram,
  finely chopped

1 teaspoon smoked sweet paprika

3 tablespoons olive oil,
  plus extra for greasing

salt and freshly ground black
  pepper, to taste

400g can black beans,
  drained and rinsed

200g sweetcorn

6 corn tortillas

2 teaspoons dried chilli flakes

330ml passata

caster sugar, to taste

70g sharp Cheddar cheese,
  coarsely grated

70g mozzarella cheese,
  torn into small strips

SERVES 6

Enchiladas get a bad wrap (tee hee). They are so often cast off as a midweek, student-style, throw-together mess without being celebrated for what they actually could be.

Enchiladas are super-filling – much more so than tacos or fajitas because they are fully wrapped up, smothered in sauce and baked with cheese. Which means they are fantastic to fill with all kinds of veggie treats. So much vegetarian food is either a sad excuse for a side dish or just not enough to keep you going, but these fellas are a great solution.

----

❶ Preheat the oven to 200°C/gas mark 6. Lightly grease a roasting tin, large enough to hold six rolled tortillas.

❷ Put the onion, carrots, squash and garlic in a separate roasting tin. Toss evenly with the marjoram, paprika, olive oil, salt and black pepper, and roast for 20–25 minutes until the squash is tender. Remove and leave to cool.

❸ Stir the black beans and sweetcorn into the squash mixture. Divide the filling equally between the tortillas, rolling each one up and placing it in the greased tin.

❹ Mix together the chilli flakes, passata and a touch of salt, black pepper and sugar, to taste. Spread over the tortillas and sprinkle with both types of cheese.

❺ Bake for 20 minutes until the cheese has melted and slightly browned. Serve immediately and devour with speed.

PLANTAIN TACOS WITH PINK PICKLED ONIONS AND QUESO FRESCO

FOR THE PINK PICKLED ONIONS

1 small red onion,
   finely sliced into half moons
55ml red wine vinegar
salt and freshly ground black
   pepper, to taste

FOR THE TACOS

4 plantains (or sweet potatoes
   if you can't get hold of
   plantains)
1 teaspoon dried chilli flakes
salt and freshly ground black
   pepper, to taste
1 tablespoon clear honey
50ml soured cream
¼ teaspoon smoked sweet paprika
16 mini corn tortillas
100g feta cheese, crumbled
a small bunch of fresh
   coriander, roughly chopped,
   to serve

SERVES 8

Plantains, or the muscly older brother of the banana, are a brilliant alternative to other starchy vegetables in a non-meat main. They have a touch of sweetness and roast perfectly.

If you want to be really authentic you can use a true *queso fresco*, but if you're feeling a little lazier, feta is a great substitute. Just crumble it over right at the end to give you a salty hit of flavour.

❶ To make the pink pickled onions, put the red onion and red wine vinegar in a small bowl and leave to macerate for 15–20 minutes while you prepare the rest of the recipe. Season with salt and black pepper and set aside.

❷ For the tacos, preheat the oven to 200°C/gas mark 6. Top and tail the plantains and then run a knife down the length of them to remove the skin. Cut the plantains into batons, about 6cm long, lengthways. Place in a roasting tray with the chilli flakes, salt and black pepper, and roast for 20–25 minutes until golden and tender. Drizzle the honey over the plantains and return to the oven for a further 5 minutes.

❸ Mix together the soured cream and paprika before assembling the tacos. Drain the pickled onions and place a spoonful onto each tortilla first, top with a handful of plantain, a snowfall of feta, a generous spoonful of soured cream and lastly, a sprinkling of coriander.

GREEN GODDESS QUESADILLAS

FOR THE QUESADILLAS

----

a large handful of fresh
   basil leaves
a large handful of fresh
   coriander
1 garlic clove, crushed
1 tablespoon pine nuts
5 tablespoons extra virgin
   olive oil
4 flour tortillas
150g frozen peas, thawed
90g green beans, trimmed
1 ripe avocado, cut in half
   and stone removed
40g Cheddar cheese,
   coarsely grated
salt and freshly ground
   black pepper, to taste
soured cream, to serve

SERVES 2

So many food cultures around the world have what is,
essentially, a kind of toastie as part of their national
table. In large parts of the US, you'll find the grilled cheese
– a beauty of simplicity and the saviour of many late-night
hunger attacks. In Italy, say hello to the panino. And in
Mexico, the quesadilla.

The fact that all these sandwiches tend to have some form
of melted cheese in them makes me very happy indeed and seems
to be something of a life lesson we could all take and learn
from. Melted cheese can unite all, sooner or later.

----

❶ Blitz the basil leaves, coriander leaves and stalks, garlic,
   pine nuts and olive oil in a small food processor until you
   have a sort of Mexican pesto.

❷ Blanch the beans in boiling salted water for 2 minutes, then
   plunge into ice-cold water to stop the cooking process.
   Spread the pesto on one half of each tortilla. Pile up
   with the peas, green beans and a scoop of avocado. Don't
   overfill the quesadillas or they will fall apart on cooking.

❸ Sprinkle each half with cheese, season and fold into
   a half moon. Place the quesadillas in a hot, dry frying
   pan and cook for 1–2 minutes on each side, until they are
   a beautiful golden brown and the cheese is just starting
   to melt.

❹ Remove from the pan and cut each one into three wedges.
   Dip into cooling soured cream to serve.

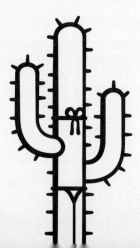

QUESO AHUMADO

FOR THE QUESO

----

1 tablespoon olive oil

1 small onion, finely diced

1 garlic clove, crushed

1 red chilli, finely diced

¼ teaspoon ground cumin

good grating of whole nutmeg

60ml milk

45ml double cream

150g smoked cheese
    (Wyke Farm smoked cheese
    works fabulously), grated

45g mozzarella cheese,
    roughly torn

salt and white pepper,
    to taste

tortilla chips, to serve

SERVES 6 (AS A SIDE)

Queso is a kind of Mexican fondue meets chip dip meets béchamel sauce that is truly, truly delightful. It is usually made from quite fresh, young, white cheese and goes by the name of *queso blanco* – often as a buddy to guac or house salsa as a little appetiser at dinner.

I like to use a really punchy smoked cheese to give it all some oomph. You need a cheese that will melt well and not go too stringy – the mozzarella will take care of that – because otherwise you'll be left fishing around the bowl for days without anything actually sticking to whatever you're dipping.

----

❶ Heat the oil in a medium saucepan. Sauté the onion until just starting to caramelise on the edges and then add the garlic and chilli, cooking for a further minute.

❷ Add the cumin and nutmeg to the pan, and heat until aromatic. Pour in the milk, cream and smoked cheese, whisking constantly over a medium heat. Once the cheese has started to melt and the queso has thickened slightly, remove it from the heat and throw in the mozzarella. It will go stringy almost immediately, so make sure you have your serving bowl ready.

❸ Add a touch of salt and white pepper and serve with a mountain of tortilla chips.

CHICHARRONES

FOR THE CHICHARRONES

760g pig skin (belly skin is
the easiest to get hold of)
4 tablespoons sea salt,
plus extra for sprinkling
1.5 litres peanut oil or
vegetable oil, for frying

SERVES 4 (AS A BEER SNACK)

Chicharrones or pork scratchings or cracklings, if you're from
the Deep South, or crispy pig skin if you are a little more
literal, are things of pure joy. They are snacking perfection
– a little salty, a little crunchy and a whole lot delicious.

I've heard a tonne of ways to make the perfect chicharron
but the trick is to take your time; these treats will not be
rushed, so be prepared to invest emotionally and hourly in
them. On the plus side, you will make the lightest, puffiest,
crispiest snack, with just a hint of porkiness. Divine.

❶ Trim the skin of any nipples (that bit always makes me
wince), or excess fat and flesh. Cut the skin in half and
place it in a large pan of cold water. Bring to the boil
and cook for 40–50 minutes at an aggressive boil. You may
need to top up the water as it evaporates.

❷ Preheat the oven to 130°C/gas mark 1. Remove the skin from
the water and leave to cool slightly. Using a sharp knife,
trim off the excess fat and flesh that may still be clinging
to the underside of the skin. Then score the skin and place
on a wire rack over a roasting tin.

❸ Rub the salt generously into the skin, then bake for at
least 2 hours, or until it has almost fully dried out and
looks like dark-brown leather.

❹ Heat the oil in a large, heavy-bottomed saucepan. Cut the
chicharrones into smaller pieces, about 4cm long. You may
have to crack the skin into shards, a bit like you would
a crab shell using the heel of your knife if it has really
dehydrated well.

❺ Test the oil is hot by dropping a small piece of skin in.
If it is hot enough it will puff up and turn almost white
in colour after a few seconds. Fry the chicharrones for
about 10 seconds, in batches, drain on kitchen paper and
sprinkle generously with extra salt. These are unbelievably
moreish dunked into some Green tomatillo salsa or Salsa roja
(page 132).

COCONUT PRAWN TOSTADAS WITH RADISH CEVICHE

FOR THE TOSTADAS

300ml vegetable oil, for frying
8 mini corn tortillas
75g plain flour
2 eggs, lightly beaten
110g desiccated coconut
½ teaspoon smoked hot paprika
200g raw king prawns, shelled
   and deveined

FOR THE CEVICHE

----

1 small red onion,
   finely sliced into half moons
150g radishes, finely sliced
juice of 2 limes
salt and freshly ground
   black pepper, to taste
1 teaspoon clear honey
3 tablespoons extra virgin
   olive oil
a small handful of fresh mint,
   finely chopped
a small handful of fresh
   coriander, finely chopped
soured cream, to serve

SERVES 4

These tostadas always remind me of my mum. Whenever we travel together in the States, usually to Florida, we have to, without fail, eat at a Bubba Gump's Shrimp Co. It's one of those traditions with no founding meaning and yet almost religious importance. Every time I order the coconut shrimp. The sweet, crunchy, hearty coating and juicy, tender prawn is just too delicious for words, and so there was no way I wasn't putting that in a recipe.

The ceviche here is not a true ceviche but rather using the acidity from the lime juice to soften the raw, wafer-thin radishes and red onion. The result is a bowl of glowing pink goodness that cuts through the sweet, creamy coconut.

----

❶ To make the tostadas, heat the oil in a large, high-sided frying pan. Test the oil is hot enough by holding the edge of a tortilla in it. If it sizzles fiercely right away, then slip in one tortilla at a time and cook for about 15 seconds per side. The tortilla will turn golden brown, magically transforming into a tostada. Drain on kitchen paper.

❷ Now make the ceviche. Mix together the onion, radishes and lime juice in a large bowl. Season with salt, black pepper and the honey, and set aside.

❸ In three separate bowls place the flour, beaten eggs and coconut mixed with the paprika. Make sure the oil you used to fry the tortillas in is still hot before dipping the prawns first in the flour, then the beaten eggs, then the coconut mixture to coat. Fry the prawns for about 1 minute until cooked all the way through – cut into one to check. Drain on kitchen paper and sprinkle with salt.

❹ Finish off the ceviche with the olive oil, mint and coriander before piling it high, with the prawns, on top of the tostadas. Crown it all with a dollop of soured cream.

POSOLE SALAD

1 dried habanero chilli

850g can white hominy

1 tablespoon vegetable oil

salt and freshly ground
  black pepper, to taste

40g salted butter

470g watermelon flesh
  (about ¼ small melon),
  cut into 2cm cubes

1 cucumber, halved, deseeded
  and cut into pieces on the
  diagonal

4 spring onions, cut into
  pieces on the diagonal

1 ripe avocado, halved, stoned
  and cut into 2cm cubes

2 tablespoons white wine
  vinegar

5 tablespoons extra virgin
  olive oil

a large handful of fresh mint,
  roughly chopped

150g feta cheese, crumbled

SERVES 6-8 (AS A SIDE)

Posole in its truest sense is a literal translation of
'hominy' – a type of large kernel corn native to the USA.
In its more common culinary sense, it is a kind of soup–stew
collaboration, made with pork, chilli and topped with avocado
or lime.

Hominy has a slightly more beany flavour than regular
sweetcorn, with much larger kernels, making this salad most
definitely not the kind you would find on a fashion magazine
editor's desk at lunchtime, next to a coconut water and a
nagging sense of desire for a cheeseburger. It is, however,
perfect for summer barbecues or any outdoor eating.

❶ Put the habanero in a bowl of boiling water. Leave for
20 minutes, then remove and finely chop.

❷ Drain and rinse the hominy before drying well with kitchen
paper. Heat the vegetable oil in a large frying pan and add
the chilli and hominy. Season well and fry for 5–7 minutes,
until warmed through. Finish with the butter and leave to
cool slightly in the pan.

❸ Put the watermelon, cucumber, spring onions and avocado in
a large bowl. Toss with a little of the white wine vinegar
to prevent the avo going brown. Add the hominy mixture to
the bowl, along with the extra virgin olive oil, remaining
vinegar, the mint, salt and black pepper, and mix well.

❹ Top with the crumbled feta and enjoy. Perfect with
a barbecue.

FOOLPROOF GUACAMOLE

FOR THE GUACAMOLE

----

2 large ripe avocados

juice of 1 lime

1 small red onion, finely diced

1 garlic clove, crushed

6 cherry tomatoes, quartered

1 red chilli, finely diced

a small handful of fresh
   coriander, roughly chopped

salt and freshly ground black
   pepper, to taste

Pictured overleaf

SERVES 2-4 (DEPENDING ON GREED)

There is nothing more glorious, more addictive, more crave-worthy than a good guac. Can you even bring yourself to imagine the travesty it would be to have dry tortilla chips?! Sitting all alone, with no cooling, creamy, tart guac to dive into? It's like ice cream without sprinkles. It shouldn't happen. And if it does, it's wrong.

I like to judge my snacks based on how well I can make them hungover and a decent bowl of guacamole is definitely do-able while still wearing last night's disco pants with eyelashes falling off your face. Trust me.

----

❶ Cut the avocados in half, remove the stones and scoop the flesh into a large bowl. Cover with the lime juice to stop it from going brown and add the onion too.

❷ Mix in the garlic and tomatoes. I like to use cherry tomatoes because you don't need to deseed them and they have a sumptuously sweet flavour.

❸ Pop the chilli into the mix with the coriander, salt and black pepper. Using your hands, squish and squelch the guacamole until it is fairly smooth but still with some chunky texture. Transfer to a slightly less messy bowl and serve, well, with anything.

SALSA ROJA

----

4 plum tomatoes, halved

1 red chilli, roughly chopped

½ red onion, roughly diced

1 tablespoon fresh marjoram

1 tablespoon cumin seeds

1 tablespoon coriander seeds

4 tablespoons olive oil

1 tablespoon caster sugar

2 garlic cloves, crushed

juice of ½ lime

2 tablespoons tomato purée

salt and freshly ground black
   pepper, to taste

tortilla chips, to serve

SERVES 6 (AS A SIDE)

True Mexican salsa is fresh, fiery and unashamedly addictive.
I've read a lot of different recipes for red salsa which range
from blitzing up the raw ingredients, to roasting everything
whole, to adding molasses for stickiness and depth. But this
combo has a lovely balance. New Mexico in a bowl.

----

❶ Preheat the oven to 200°C/gas mark 6. Spread the tomatoes
   over a baking tray. Add the chilli, onion, marjoram, cumin
   seeds, coriander seeds and olive oil, and toss together.
   Roast for 15–20 minutes until slightly caramelised.

❷ Blitz the roasted tomato mix, sugar, garlic, lime juice,
   tomato purée and salt and black pepper in a blender until
   as smooth as possible.

❸ Decant the salsa into a bowl and serve with tortilla chips.

GREEN TOMATILLO SALSA

FOR THE SALSA

500g fresh tomatillos

2 green chillies

1 garlic clove, peeled

3 spring onions

a large handful of coriander

1½ teaspoons caster

salt and freshly ground
   black pepper, to taste

tortilla chips, to serve

SERVES 6 (AS A SIDE)

If you've never seen a tomatillo, you could easily be forgiven
for thinking you are looking at a slightly peaky tomato.
Tomatillos are not in fact green tomatoes but are a slightly
different being covered in a papery husk, with a more citrusy-
fruity flavour.

----

❶ Remove the outer leaves and stalks from the tomatillos
   and put in a wide, shallow, dry frying pan with the
   chillies. Scorch over a high heat for 10–12 minutes
   until they are blistered and blackened.

❷ Cut the stalks off the chillies and split them down the
   middle. Remove the seeds and put in a food processor with
   the garlic, spring onions, coriander, sugar, salt and black
   pepper. Blitz, add three tomatillos at a time and blitz
   again: adding them in batches ensures a smoother sauce.

❸ Taste and add a little more sugar if it is too sharp,
   or salt if it is a bit bland. Pour into a large bowl
   and serve alongside an enormous bowl of tortilla chips.

BAKING
AND
Su

Someone once told me that the smell of vanilla, particularly the smell of vanilla when used in baking, has been scientifically proven to make people happier. It's something to do with them associating the smell with childhood memories of baking with their grandma, or something along those lines.

My grandma never used to bake with us but gave us Chinese takeaway, chips and Wagon Wheels instead, which, in my view, made her both badass and ahead of her time. So while I might not associate vanilla smells with memories of happy families and childhood, I still love it more than I can say, so those scientists must be on to something.

Baking is such an institution in the States that it's hard to pick a shortlist of recipes that show it off properly, but I think this chapter offers a pretty good representation. You've got the diner desserts of the South with Lemon chess pie (page 150) as well as pure New-England treats like Chocolate peppermint whoopie pies (page 143) or Boston cream pie (page 145). Baking is the ultimate expression of comfort – both in the fact that it is in and of itself a comfort food and that so many of these sweet treats are twisted and transformed versions of their European ancestors. Immigrants to the States would bake as a way of strengthening their cultural roots, which in turn created cookies, cakes and pies that were more American than ever. There may be nothing more American than apple pie, but that's probably because that pie was originally French or German or Austrian and got twisted, tweaked and transformed into something uniquely of the U.S. of A.

When it comes to baking, I can see why many people would rather find a nice bakery, where they also do takeaway coffee and free wifi, rather than whipping out measuring spoons and myriad of cake tins. Coming from one of the laziest people in the world, who often considers getting dressed an unnecessary formality on a Sunday, take it from me, I hear you. And there are some things that professional bakers, or baking nerds, do better because of their experience.

So that is why all the recipes in this chapter are very much ones that I think baking should be about. They are all pretty much these two things: 1) Straightforward, with minimal faffing about and convenient tin shapes to line (if you've ever tried to line a bundt tin, you will know what I'm talking about); and 2) They are all balanced in flavour.

Things like herbs or salt can take the edge off something on the verge of becoming sickly sweet and give it another dimension that lifts the whole bake. I don't have an overly sweet tooth, so cakes that are pure sugar with nothing else to bring to the party really bore me. They leave you feeling droopy, tired and worst of all, sick. No dessert should ever make you feel like you would have been better off without it. You should only feel that way if you make like a truffling pig and gorge on half the brownie pan in one go. Been there, my friend. Beeeeeen there.

KEY LIME PIE

FOR THE PIE

100g ginger nut biscuits
150g digestive biscuits
125g salted butter, melted
397g can condensed milk
4 egg yolks
zest of 5 limes
juice of 2 limes
1 tablespoon white rum
  (optional)
250ml double cream
1 tablespoon icing sugar

SERVES 6

I've lived in Florida twice and it's probably my favourite place. It has some of the most diverse food scenes I've ever come across — from Cuban stews and sandwiches in Little Havana to Jamaican home cooking and everything in between.

Key lime pie is a fantastic example of this. Key limes are a type of lime found on the Keys that are about one-third of the size of what we know as regular limes... or Persian limes if you want to give them their true jazzy name. They have a stronger smell and punchier acidity, and make for the most gorgeous, sharp, creamy dessert known on either side of the Atlantic.

---

❶ Preheat the oven to 190°C/gas mark 5. Blitz the ginger nut and digestive biscuits in a food processor until really fine. Stir through the melted butter and tip into a 22cm pie dish.

❷ Using your fingers, press the biscuit into the corners and up the sides of the dish to form a crust, then bake for 10 minutes. Remove from the oven and leave to cool fully.

❸ In a large bowl, beat together the condensed milk, egg yolks, lime zest and juice, and rum, if using, until you have a smooth, lime-speckled mix. Pour into the pie dish and leave to set in the fridge for a minimum of 3 hours.

❹ When the pie is set, whip the cream and icing sugar together to form soft peaks and pile high on the centre of the pie. Enjoy in hearty slices.

S'MORES CHEESECAKE

FOR THE CHEESECAKE

- -

100g whole blanched hazelnuts

250g digestive biscuits

good grating of whole nutmeg

160g salted butter, melted

100g dark chocolate
   (minimum 70 per cent
   cocoa solids), broken
   into small chunks

500g full-fat cream cheese

60g icing sugar, sifted

1 teaspoon vanilla bean
   paste or 2 teaspoons
   vanilla extract

300g Nutella

125g mini marshmallows

SERVES 8

- -

If you grew up in the States and were a member of the Girl or Boy Scouts, s'mores would have been your bread and butter — or to put it more accurately — your graham crackers, toasted marshmallow and chocolate. S'mores are a campfire necessity. Super-easy to make, dangerously delicious and seductively moreish. Their very name is a smooshing together of 'some more'. Need I say s'more?

- -

❶ Preheat the oven to 180°C/gas mark 4. Line the base of a loose-bottomed 23cm cake tin with baking parchment.

❷ Pour the hazelnuts into a dry frying pan and toast over a medium heat until golden. Tip into a food processor with the biscuits and nutmeg and blitz until the mixture resembles fine breadcrumbs.

❸ Stir the melted butter through the biscuit mix and tumble into the prepared cake tin, pressing firmly into the edges (I find a potato masher works brilliantly here). Bake the base for 15 minutes, then leave to cool completely.

❹ Melt the chocolate in a heatproof bowl set over a pan of boiling water (don't allow the base of the bowl to touch the water) then leave it to cool slightly. Meanwhile, pop the cream cheese, icing sugar, vanilla and Nutella in a bowl or freestanding mixer and beat together until smooth. You should want to jump right into that bowl and swim around devouring it all. If you don't feel that urge, keep beating.

❺ Pour in the melted chocolate, mixing constantly, then spoon the mixture on top of the biscuit base and smooth around the top. Pop the cheesecake into the fridge to set for a minimum of 3 hours, although overnight is best.

❻ Once set, arrange the marshmallows over the top and blowtorch until they are lightly scorched and take you back to nights in front of the campfire.

CHOCOLATE PEPPERMINT WHOOPIE PIES

FOR THE PIES

125g unsalted butter,
  cut into cubes
150g dark chocolate
  (minimum 70 per cent
  cocoa solids), broken
  into small chunks
220g caster sugar
3 eggs, lightly beaten
1 teaspoon vanilla bean
  paste, or 2 teaspoons
  vanilla extract
255g plain flour
20g cocoa powder
½ teaspoon baking powder
¼ teaspoon salt

FOR THE BUTTERCREAM FROSTING

250g unsalted butter, softened
500g icing sugar, sifted
2 teaspoons peppermint extract
3 tablespoons milk

MAKES 8 PIES

The story goes that Amish women — whose job it mostly was to stay at home, raising babies and baking cookies — would often have a little extra cake batter left over from a long stay at the stove and make these treats to put in their husbands' lunch boxes. The husbands would then (apparently) yell 'Whoopie!' and so, low and behold, the whoopie pie was born. Do I necessarily believe this tale? No. But I do love the idea that any grown man, Amish or not, yells 'Whoopie!' at the sign of a baked treat at lunch.

----

❶ Preheat the oven to 160°C/gas mark 3. Line a large baking tray with baking parchment.

❷ To make the pies, melt the butter and chocolate together in a heatproof bowl set over a pan of simmering water, and leave to cool slightly.

❸ In a separate bowl, whisk together the caster sugar, eggs and vanilla until light and frothy then pour the melted chocolate and butter in, whisking constantly.

❹ In a large mixing bowl, combine the flour, cocoa powder, baking powder and salt, and add to the chocolate mix a spoon at a time, making sure it is well incorporated.

❺ Using an ice cream scoop, spoon 16 even blobs of pie mix onto the prepared baking tray. The mixture will look quite loose at this point. Leave them plenty of room to grow and bake for 10–12 minutes until just cooked through. Leave to cool completely on a wire rack.

❻ Meanwhile, make the buttercream frosting. In a freestanding electric mixer, beat the butter for about 4 minutes until really soft and fluffy. Add the icing sugar and beat again, covering the machine with a tea towel to prevent icing sugar explosions. Continue beating the butter and sugar until the mixture turns white and super-soft — this can take up to 5 minutes of continuous beating interspersed with occasional spatula scraping. Add the peppermint extract and milk, and beat on a high speed until fully blended.

❼ To build each pie, pipe a liberal swoosh of frosting onto the flat side of one half. Sandwich the top with the other half, et voila, you are halfway to being Amish.

PUMPKIN PIE

FOR THE PASTRY

250g plain flour, plus extra
   for dusting
½ teaspoon salt
1 tablespoon caster sugar
2 teaspoons ground cinnamon
140g cold unsalted butter,
   cut into 1cm cubes
2 egg yolks

FOR THE FILLING

425g can pumpkin purée
2 tablespoons maple syrup
1 teaspoon ground mixed spice
½ teaspoon ground nutmeg
¼ teaspoon ground cloves
zest of 1 orange
zest of 1 lemon
3 eggs, lightly beaten
pinch of salt
100g soft light brown sugar
200ml double cream,
   plus 300ml for whipping
1 tablespoon icing sugar

SERVES 6

To those who ask the somewhat rhetorical question 'Is there anything more American than apple pie?', I challenge with a 'Yes. Yes there is. Come with me, sir, and let me show you the wonder that is pumpkin pie'.

I know it can seem weird to those who have only ever seen pumpkins hollowed out with candles in them or roasted as a savoury vegetable to imagine them in a dessert, but hear me out. Let's all think back to our old friend cheesecake and what a vast array of confused faces he faced upon arrival. And look how we love him now! It can be done. Give pies a chance.

❶ To make the pastry, blitz the flour, salt, caster sugar, cinnamon and butter in a food processor until the mixture resembles fine breadcrumbs.

❷ Tip the mixture into a large bowl and add the egg yolks and 3 tablespoons of cold water. Stir very quickly using a blunt knife and bring together with your hands. Knead quickly to make it into a flat disc, then cover with clingfilm and chill for 30 minutes.

❸ Preheat the oven to 190°C/gas mark 5. Once cold, roll the pastry out onto a lightly floured surface to 3mm thick and use it to line a 22cm pie dish. Press the pastry into the corners and cover with baking parchment. Fill with baking beans and blind bake for 20–25 minutes until cooked through on the sides. Remove the parchment and beans and cook for a further 5 minutes to dry out the base. Remove from the oven, then reduce the temperature to 160°C/gas mark 3.

❹ For the filling, mix the pumpkin purée, maple syrup, spices and zests of both fruits in a freestanding electric mixer. Add the eggs, salt and brown sugar and the 200ml of cream, mixing as you go. Pour the filling into the pastry case and bake for 40–50 minutes until the centre is set. Remove from the oven and leave to cool fully.

❺ Whip the remaining 300ml of cream with the icing sugar to pillowy, soft peaks and pile high on the centre of the pie. Serve in generous slices.

BOSTON CREAM PIE

FOR THE CAKE

4 eggs

½ teaspoon vanilla extract

125g caster sugar, plus extra
  for dusting

60g salted butter, melted
  and cooled, plus extra
  for greasing

125g plain flour, plus extra
  for dusting

FOR THE CRÈME PÂTISSIÈRE

300ml milk

3 egg yolks

1 teaspoon vanilla bean
  paste or 2 teaspoons
  vanilla extract

60g caster sugar

20g plain flour

20g cornflour

100ml double cream

FOR THE CHOCOLATE GANACHE

125ml double cream

200g dark chocolate
  (minimum 70 per cent
  cocoa solids), broken
  into small chunkss

1 tablespoon golden syrup

SERVES 6

Just to confuse you, this is a cake, not a pie. It's also the official State dessert of Massachusetts. I can't decide if I love it even more because of this or if I actually just love the fact that there are 'Official State Desserts'. One tip here, have all your ingredients measured out alongside your equipment ready to go.

❶ Preheat the oven to 180°C/gas mark 4. Grease and line a 22cm loose-bottomed cake tin and dust with a little caster sugar followed by flour.

❷ For the cake, place a heatproof bowl over a pan of simmering water. Add the eggs, vanilla and sugar, and whisk on full whack for about 5 minutes until the mixture has tripled in volume and is light and mousse-like. Remove the bowl from the pan and continue whisking until it's cool. Pour the cooled butter around the edge and fold in.

❸ Sift the flour over the top of the mixture and fold in. Again, don't wreck it by bashing away like a mad man. Fold, fold. Scrape the batter into the tin and bake for 30–35 minutes until a skewer inserted into the centre comes out clean. Leave to cool in its tin on a wire rack.

❹ Meanwhile, make the crème pâtissière. Bring the milk just to a simmer in a small saucepan, then remove from the heat. In a small bowl, mix together the egg yolks, vanilla, sugar, plain flour and cornflour. Add the warm milk, a splash at a time, beating out any lumps. Pour back into the pan and bring to the boil, whisking constantly. It will go lumpy after a minute or so, then stir it like crazy to get all the lumps out. Let it bubble for a further minute to cook out the flour. Scrape the custard into a bowl and leave to cool.

❺ Meanwhile, whip the cream to very soft, light peaks. Once the custard has cooled, whisk through the whipped cream and set aside.

❻ Now for the ganache. Boil the cream in a saucepan and put the chocolate chunks and golden syrup in a heatproof bowl. Pour over the cream and stir until the chocolate has melted and you have a gloriously glossy mixture.

❼ Split the cake in half horizontally and pile the custard onto one half, spreading to the edges. Top with the other half and pour the chocolate ganache all over the exposed surface pushing it right over the edges and letting it drip down the sides.

PEACH, ORANGE AND HONEY COBBLER

FOR THE FRUIT

411g can peach slices

500g (about 3 large) fresh
peaches, stoned and sliced
into 2cm-thick wedges

½ teaspoon ground cinnamon

100g soft light brown sugar

¼ teaspoon salt

zest of 2 oranges

juice of 1 orange

1 tablespoon semolina

FOR THE BISCUIT TOPPING

240g plain flour, plus extra
for dusting

60g granulated sugar

1½ teaspoons baking powder

85g unsalted butter,
plus extra for greasing

50g ground almonds

200ml double cream

2 tablespoons clear honey,
plus a little extra
for drizzling

SERVES 4-6

In the south, Georgia especially, where they are famous for
their glorious, gleaming peaches, cobblers come in two types.
One is cakey and almost like a sweet, fruity 'toad in the
hole', where the batter rises around the filling once in the
oven. This is the other one, with a biscuit topping, something
much more akin to a doughy scone. Proudly dotted all around
the top of the fruit, the cobbler scones scream 'Eat me now!'.

❶ Preheat the oven to 180°C/gas mark 4. Butter a 26cm square
pie or lasagne dish.

❷ To prepare the fruit, drain the tinned peaches and put in
a large mixing bowl. Add the fresh peaches. Throw in the
cinnamon, brown sugar, salt, orange zest and juice, and mix
well. There will be a deep-brown liquor in the bottom of the
bowl, with the fruit gleaming like little golden half moons
on top.

❸ Sprinkle the semolina into the prepared pie dish, covering
the base evenly, then tumble in all the fruit and liquor.

❹ Now, you're ready to make the biscuit topping. Blitz the
flour, granulated sugar, baking powder, butter and almonds
in a food processor until the mixture resembles a pale
crumble mix. Add the cream and honey, and blitz until you
have what looks like a thick cake batter.

❺ Scrape the batter out onto a floured surface, making sure
your hands are suitably dusted too. Pull off little portions
and roll gently into balls a little smaller than a tennis
ball. (I usually work to nine for a dish this size, in three
rows of three.) Place on top of the peaches, and drizzle
with a little extra honey.

❻ Bake for 40–50 minutes until all the biscuits are golden and
crunchy on top and the fruit is just bubbling through. Serve.

SALTED CARAMEL PRETZEL POUND CAKE

FOR THE CAKE

75g unsalted butter, softened,
  plus extra for greasing
200g caster sugar
150ml soured cream
2 eggs, lightly beaten
½ teaspoon vanilla bean paste
  or 1 teaspoon vanilla extract
200g plain flour
35g cocoa powder
¼ teaspoon bicarbonate of soda
¾ teaspoon baking powder
¼ teaspoon salt
30ml milk

FOR THE BUTTERCREAM FROSTING

125g unsalted butter, softened
250g icing sugar, sifted
½ teaspoon vanilla bean paste
  or 1 teaspoon vanilla extract
1½ tablespoons milk
125g small, snack-sized
  salted pretzels

FOR THE SALTED SAUCE

80g soft light brown sugar
85ml double cream
30g unsalted butter
½ teaspoon salt

SERVES 8

Okay, spoiler alert. This is not strictly a pound cake.
But, saying that, it comes pretty damn close and is a real
showstopper with minimal effort. Any cake that has an equal
proportion of sugar, flour, eggs and butter is a pound cake
as these used to be a pound (or 450g) of each. That's a *lot*
of eggs. And a lot of cake in general, which is why this one
isn't strictly a *pound* cake but it still provides you with
comfort and joy, which is its main purpose really.

❶ Preheat the oven to 180°C/gas mark 4. Grease and line
  a 22 x 11.5 x 7cm loaf tin with baking parchment.

❷ Start by making the cake. In a freestanding electric mixer
  bowl, beat together the butter and caster sugar for about
  5 minutes until light and fluffy. Mix together the soured
  cream, eggs and vanilla in a jug.

❸ In a mixing bowl, combine the flour, cocoa powder, bicarbonate
  of soda, baking powder and salt. Add the soured cream mix
  and the flour mix to the butter and sugar alternately, making
  sure to scrape down the sides of the bowl occasionally.
  Lastly, add the milk to loosen the mixture slightly, then
  scrape it into the prepared tin. Bake for 50–60 minutes
  until a skewer inserted into the centre comes out clean.
  Leave to cool in the tin on a wire rack for 10 minutes
  before turning out and leaving to cool fully.

❹ Meanwhile, make the frosting. Beat the butter in a bowl
  until soft and fluffy. Add the icing sugar and beat again
  for about 4 minutes until the frosting is bright white and
  pillowy. Add the vanilla and milk, and beat until fully
  mixed in, then set aside.

❺ To make the caramel sauce, mix all the ingredients together
  in a small pan and heat gently until the sugar has dissolved.
  Boil the caramel for 1 minute before turning off the heat
  and leaving to cool. Let it drop in temperature enough so
  that you have a thick, drizzle-able sauce.

❻ To frost the cake, spread a generous amount of the frosting
  over the top of the loaf and arrange the pretzels on top.
  Drizzle with the salted caramel sauce before serving in
  hearty slabs.

LEMON CHESS PIE

FOR THE PASTRY

250g plain flour, plus extra
  for dusting

2 tablespoons caster sugar

pinch of salt

140g cold unsalted butter,
  cut into 1cm cubes

2 egg yolks

FOR THE FILLING

160g caster sugar

50g plain flour

1 tablespoon fine ground
  cornmeal

4 eggs

60g salted butter,
  melted and cooled

160ml double cream

juice and zest of 3 lemons

SERVES 6

The story behind the beginnings of the lemon chess pie is about as charming as any Southern gentleman. Apparently, a woman walked into a diner and asked her waitress what desserts were on that day. The server, in her thick South Carolina accent replied 'Just pie' which sounded to the Yankee diner like 'Chess Pie', which she ordered, loved and the name stuck.

Lemon chess pie is very similar to a French tarte au citron, with its citrus-cream filling, but has a spoonful of cornmeal for added bite and a cloud of whipped cream for good measure.

❶ To make the pastry, blitz the flour, sugar, salt and butter in a food processor until the mixture resembles fine breadcrumbs.

❷ Tip into a large bowl and add the egg yolks and 3 tablespoons of cold water. Stir together very quickly using a blunt knife, then bring together with your hands. Give the pastry a good, quick knead to make it into a flat disc, then cover with clingfilm and chill for 30 minutes.

❸ Preheat the oven to 190°C/gas mark 5. Once cold, roll the pastry out on a lightly floured surface to 3mm thick and use it to line a 22cm pie dish. Press well into the corners and cover with baking parchment. Fill with baking beans and blind bake for 20–25 minutes until cooked through on the sides. Remove the parchment and beans and cook for a further 5 minutes to dry out the base. Remove from the oven and reduce the temperature to 170°C/gas mark 3.

❹ For the filling, mix the sugar, flour and cornmeal together well. Add the eggs one at a time, beating well after each addition. Pour in the melted butter, cream and lemon juice and zest. The mixture will look quite loose. Pour the filling into the pastry case and bake for 35–40 minutes until the centre is set. If the crust begins to look a little dark partway through, cover it with foil and return to the oven.

❺ Leave the tart to cool before slicing and eating; this is best eaten just a little warm.

STRAWBERRY AND BASIL SHORTCAKES

FOR THE SHORTCAKES

310g plain flour, plus extra
  for dusting
½ teaspoon salt
1 tablespoon baking powder
50g caster sugar
150g unsalted butter,
  cut into 1cm cubes
1 egg
150ml double cream
1 teaspoon vanilla bean
  paste, or 2 teaspoons
  vanilla extract
1 egg yolk, for glazing
1 tablespoon milk, for glazing

FOR THE STRAWBERRY FILLING

400g strawberries, hulled
  and chopped into quarters,
  plus 200g strawberries,
  hulled and sliced
50g caster sugar
a small handful of fresh
  basil leaves, thinly sliced
250ml double cream
2 tablespoons icing sugar

MAKES 8 SHORTCAKES

I don't have the world's biggest sweet tooth, so the herbaceous hint in these shortcakes suits me down to the ground. They are sweet, obviously, but the aromatic basil just takes the edge off them being too saccharine.

Shortcakes are a kind of sconey cake, where you don't overwork the dough and keep the butter cold so that the final cakes are super-flaky, tender and… well… short. Pile them high with fruit, whipped cream and more whipped cream until they are so tall you can't see over the top of them.

❶ Preheat the oven to 190°C/gas mark 5. Line a baking tray with baking parchment. To make the shortcakes, blitz the flour, salt, baking powder, sugar and butter in a food processor until the mixture resembles fine breadcrumbs.

❷ In a jug, whisk together the egg, cream and vanilla, and with the motor still running, add this to the flour mix. Once it has come together, turn out onto a floured surface and knead lightly to form a smooth dough.

❸ Roll the dough out to 2cm thick and, using a 9cm cookie cutter, stamp out eight shortcakes. You may need to re-roll the dough in between cuts. Place the shortcakes on the prepared baking tray, leaving room for them to grow.

❹ Mix together the egg yolk and milk for glazing and brush the top of each cake. Bake for 20–25 minutes until cooked through and golden – they should have a natural crack along their middles. Transfer to a wire rack and leave to cool.

❺ For the strawberry filling, put 400g of strawberries, the caster sugar and 140ml of cold water in a saucepan and bring to a simmer. Give the strawberries a good mush occasionally to soften. Once the sauce has simmered for about 10 minutes, blitz well and pass through a fine sieve to remove any seeds. Then pop it into a clean bowl and stir through the basil and the remaining 200g of strawberries.

❻ Whip the cream and icing sugar together until you have soft peaks. Split each cake in half along its middle, using that natural crack as a guide. Spread one half with a generous spoonful of strawberry sauce and a healthy dollop of whipped cream. Top with the other half and devour with glee.

RED VELVET BIRTHDAY CAKE

FOR THE CAKE

390g plain flour
290g caster sugar
1 tablespoon baking powder
½ teaspoon salt
3 tablespoons cocoa powder
½ teaspoon bicarbonate of soda
245ml soured cream
2 eggs
1 teaspoon white wine vinegar
1 tablespoon red food
    colouring gel
1 teaspoon vanilla bean
    paste, or 2 teaspoons
    vanilla extract
240ml vegetable oil,
    plus extra for greasing

FOR THE CREAM CHEESE FROSTING

300g unsalted butter, softened
300g icing sugar, sifted
½ teaspoon vanilla extract
840g full-fat cream cheese

SERVES 8

A lot of people think that red velvet is a true Southern recipe but there's no definitive proof that it was invented in the South. You can get phenomenal red velvets all over the US which all contain some of the same key ingredients to make them a little bit special. The vinegar cuts through the rich taste and the touch of cocoa powder makes the cake incredibly rich and decadent without being an out and out chocolate cake.

And then, there's the colour. You must use a concentrated food colouring gel here and not any cheap crap from the 'Home Baking' aisle of your local supermarket. It will be far too watery and weak, leaving you with something more appropriately titled 'Sludge brown velvet cake'.

---

❶ Preheat the oven to 180°C/gas mark 4. Grease and line two 23cm loose-bottomed cake tins with baking parchment.

❷ To make the cake, mix the flour, caster sugar, baking powder, salt, cocoa powder and bicarbonate of soda in a freestanding electric mixer bowl.

❸ In a separate jug, put the soured cream, eggs, vinegar, food colouring and vanilla. With the motor running, add the oil to the flour mix and beat until mixed in. Then add the soured cream and egg mix and beat until you have a smooth, flowing batter. Divide the batter between the cake tins and smooth out on top. Bake for 22–25 minutes until a skewer inserted into the middle comes out clean. Leave the cakes to cool in their tins for 10 minutes, then release them and leave to cool fully.

❹ For the cream cheese frosting, beat the butter in a freestanding electric mixer bowl for about 5 minutes until really soft. Then sift in the icing sugar and beat again until smooth and mixed in. (The sugar can go flying at this point so cover the machine with a tea towel.) Next, mix in the vanilla and lastly stir in the cream cheese. Don't overmix as it can become very runny, very quickly.

❺ Once the cakes have cooled, trim the tops to make a flat surface and place one layer on a plate. Spread a generous amount of frosting on top and crown with the second layer. Spread the remaining cream cheese frosting all over the top and sides before diving in.

SNICKERDOODLES

FOR THE COOKIES

150g unsalted butter, softened
80g soft light brown sugar
80g caster sugar
1 teaspoon vanilla bean
  paste, or 2 teaspoons
  vanilla extract
1 egg
225g plain flour
½ teaspoon bicarbonate of soda
¼ teaspoon salt

FOR THE CINNAMON SUGAR

1½ teaspoons ground cinnamon
100g golden caster sugar

MAKES 8 GIGANTIC COOKIES

Snickerdoodles are a cinnamon-rolled sugar cookie popular all over the States but particularly in New England. Their name has a history that is so much greater than just someone thinking up a kooky term. 'Schneckennudel', which translates as 'snail cookie' because of its swirly shape, is a kind of German cinnamon bun. German immigrants to Pennsylvania and New England brought with them their luggage, their dreams of a new life and most importantly (I mean, I never travel without these) their baked goods. The name went through the Chinese whispers chain and came out as 'Snickerdoodle'.

These cookies are characteristically fluffier than a traditional chocolate chip. They are also gigantic, so this batch only really makes eight cowpat-sized cookies. If you want to make mini ones, just bake them for 5 minutes to keep them soft in the middle. And *please* call them Snickerdoodlettes.

---

❶ Preheat the oven to 180°C/gas mark 4. Line 2 large baking trays with baking parchment. To make the cookies, beat together the butter and both sugars in a freestanding electric mixer for about 5 minutes until light and fluffy. Scrape down the sides regularly using a spatula.

❷ Add the vanilla and egg, and beat again until fully incorporated. Sift in the flour, bicarbonate of soda and salt, and stir gently to bring everything together.

❸ For the cinnamon sugar, mix together the cinnamon and sugar in a small bowl. Divide the cookie dough into eight even-sized pieces. Roll each piece into a ball and coat fully in cinnamon sugar.

❹ Place four cookie balls onto each prepared tray, leaving space for them to spread. Gently press each ball until it's flat and about 1cm thick.

❺ Bake for 12–15 minutes until golden and slightly cracked on top. Transfer to a wire rack and leave to cool, then dip into glasses of ice-cold milk to eat.

PINK GRAPEFRUIT CAKE

FOR THE CAKE

350g unsalted butter, softened,
  plus extra for greasing
350g caster sugar
5 eggs, lightly beaten
350g self-raising flour
2 teaspoons baking powder
pinch of salt
1 teaspooon vanilla bean
  paste or 2 teaspoons
  vanilla extract
zest of 2 pink grapefruits
5 tablespoons pink grapefruit
  juice

FOR THE FROSTING

300g unsalted butter, softened
300g icing sugar, sifted
840g full-fat cream cheese
zest of 2 pink grapefruits
½ teaspoon vanilla extract
touch of tangerine food
  colouring

SERVES 8-10

When I was twenty, I spent a summer working at Walt Disney World in Florida. There was a restaurant in the park modelled after the Hollywood Brown Derby in, well, Hollywood. This restaurant (the real one) used to be *the* place where all the movie stars would hang out. I never went to the real one, most likely because I wasn't a 1930s starlet, but the one in Florida was my dream eatery. One of the signature dishes from the Derby (the real and the pretend one) was their grapefruit cake, made for an unnamed actress who wanted cake but still wanted something healthy with fruit in it. I may not have eaten at that fancy restaurant all that much, but I can have the cake any time I want.

----

❶ Preheat the oven to 190°C/gas mark 5. Grease and line two 22cm loose-bottomed cake tins with baking parchment.

❷ For the cake, beat together the butter and caster sugar in a freestanding electric mixer for about 5 minutes until light and fluffy. Add the eggs a little at a time, beating well after each addition to make sure they are fully incorporated.

❸ Mix the flour, baking powder and salt together in a bowl and add this to the butter mixture a spoonful at a time. Lastly, add the vanilla, grapefruit zest and juice. Divide the batter equally between the cake tins, smooth the tops and bake for 25–30 minutes until golden on top and a skewer inserted into the centre comes out clean. Leave the cakes to cool in their tins for 10 minutes before releasing them and letting them cool completely on wire racks.

❹ To make the frosting, beat the butter in a bowl for about 4 minutes until utterly soft and yielding. Then add the icing sugar, covering the bowl with a tea towel before beating in well. Continue mixing until it turns white and fluffy, which can take up to 5 minutes. Turn the cream cheese through the mixture, combining thoroughly before mixing in the zest, vanilla and food colouring. The mixture should turn the kind of colour you might call 'Tangerine Dream'.

❺ Lay the first layer of cake on a board and spread a liberal amount of frosting on top, right to the edges. Top this with the second layer, bottom-side facing up so that you have a completely flat surface on the top of the cake. Frost all over the top and sides of the cake with the remaining frosting, and dig in. Ideally with a large pot of fresh coffee nearby.

BLACK CHERRY AND CHOCOLATE CUPCAKES

FOR THE CUPCAKES

120g dried sour cherries
400ml just-boiled water
200g plain flour
50g cocoa powder
1½ teaspoons instant
  espresso powder
1 tablespoon baking powder
¼ teaspoon salt
80g unsalted butter, softened
280g caster sugar
2 eggs, lightly beaten
1 teaspoon vanilla bean
  paste or 2 teaspoons
  vanilla extract
200ml milk

FOR THE FROSTING

250g unsalted butter, softened
500g icing sugar, sifted
2 teaspoons Kirsch
3 tablespoons milk
purple and red food
  colouring gels

MAKES 12 CUPCAKES

Some things may be retro but they are legendary for a reason. Legwarmers? Yes. Wham? So many hits. Black Forest gateau? Please, pass me a fork and don't move me from this sofa. Cherries and chocolate are just dreamy together. Just a smidge of liquor makes these extra-delicious with a rich, cocoa-heavy base — you can't go wrong.

❶ Preheat the oven to 180°C/gas mark 4. Line a 12-hole cupcake tin with paper cases.

❷ For the cupcakes, soak the cherries in the just-boiled water for 20 minutes. Meanwhile, mix together the flour, cocoa, espresso and baking powders and salt in a large bowl.

❸ In a freestanding electric mixer, beat togethe the butter and caster sugar for about 5 minutes until light and fluffy. Scrape down the sides occasionally. Add the eggs a little at a time, whisking well after each addition. Add the vanilla and then alternate with spoonfuls of the dry ingredients and milk, whisking until you have a smooth, thick batter.

❹ Drain the cherries from their water and roughly chop them. Stir through the batter and then divide between the cupcake cases. I find an ice-cream scoop with a scraping attachment is best here. Failing that, just make sure you only fill the cases about two-thirds full. Bake for 15–20 minutes until a skewer inserted into the centre of the cakes comes out clean. Leave the cupcakes to cool fully on a wire rack while you make the frosting.

❺ Beat the butter in a bowl for about 4 minutes until soft and fluffy. Add the icing sugar and beat again for a further 4 minutes until the frosting is bright-white and pillowy. Pour in the Kirsch and milk, and beat until fully mixed. Stir through a mixture of purple and red food colouring to make a vibrant, cherry-red colour — but go little by little. Food colouring gel packs a punch, so you won't need much.

❻ Spread the frosting on the cupcakes any way you like. You could use a piping bag and go mad with your nozzle selection... or... you could be like me and indulge in the rustic approach. Simply smoosh a generous blob onto the top of each cake. Maybe decorate with a sprinkle or two. The decorating cupboard is your oyster.

DRI
&

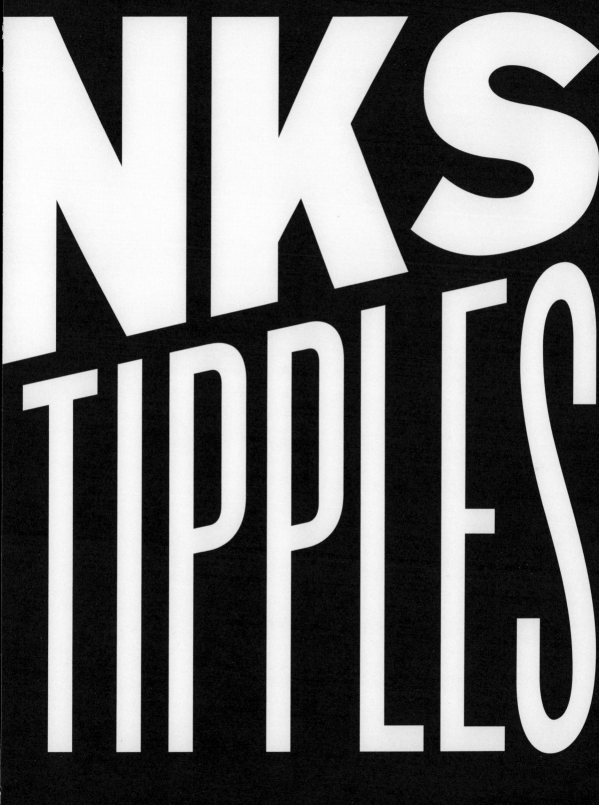

There is something so special about a cocktail and I don't know what it is. Maybe it's the fact that it takes about three times as long to make as pouring a glass of wine, so you have to wait a little, like a really hot date where you don't want to seem too keen but are itching with nerves and rage that he's late.

Or maybe it's because they usually have a hefty price tag attached to them, so we feel we are treating ourselves. Or it could be that they all seem to have a real back-story. Like any good movie, they have fascinating histories and origins, which make them that little bit special. They deserve to be celebrated, so let's drink.

America is a cocktail nation. It's written in its literature, in its movies, in its very core. The fact that Prohibition happened just goes to show how liquor and the beauties it can be mixed to make are a lot more powerful than they may at first appear. Can you imagine reading *The Great Gatsby* without Manhattan and Long Island Ice Teas? Or listening to Willie Nelson and not hearing 'Whiskey River'? Or watching any teen movie where the prom punch isn't spiked?! To imagine America without cocktails and drinks would be to imagine somewhere missing a huge part of its culture and heritage. Or to imagine Utah.

History lives on through food, but it also lives on through drink, and these recipes are testimony to that. Their names are a wonderful mix of quirk and legacy, and were often the creations of bartenders much more skilled than I ever was. I doubt they ever hid in the cellar for 30 minutes, trying to avoid doing any work on a shift. And they all knew how to make a cocktail like most of us know how to make fried eggs or a cup of coffee. It was second nature to them, and hugely special to us.

People like Jerry Thomas who published *Bartenders Guide* in 1862 gave us drinks that still taste divine and knock us for six. I think these guys deserve more recognition – how many break-ups, bad days at work and birthdays have they got us through? The world would be a much sadder place without gin fizzes, Tom Collins' and bloody Marys, so let's raise a literal and metaphorical glass to those people who have made us tipsy for centuries. Salud!

A note on jam-jar cocktails

I don't know about you, but I have a real Jekyll-and-Hyde attitude towards spending money on kitchen gadgets and equipment. Part of me SO wants it that the price is a mere temporary barrier and then another part of me is screaming 'NO! FLO, NO! PUT THE WALLET AWAY! HAVE A CHEESEBURGER AND CALM DOWN'. Things like ice-cream makers, for instance, I feel that I have to have, because just think of all the flavours you could make and how smooth and creamy it would be if you had the right tools for the job! And then BAM! It's sitting in the back of the cabinet next to the melon ballers and sushi rolling mats.

Cocktail shakers and all the paraphernalia that goes along with them fit this exact gadgetry genre. If you are super into cocktails and have one every night with dinner – firstly, where's my invite to this daily party? – then by all means invest in the best and have that jigger and muddler to hand.

On the other hand, if you are trying to be frugal and kick the late-night online bits and bobs shopping habit, then a large jam jar, long spoon and small sieve will do the job perfectly well. These recipes are designed to be made with what you have to hand in the house and taste damn fine just the same.

A note on recipe amounts

Cocktails are mostly all about proportions of ingredients, so almost all the recipes in this chapter are for one drink. I cannot do maths for the life of me, so I find this is by far the easiest way to multiply for as many cocktails as you would like.

GRACE'S GREYHOUND

----

crushed ice,
  to fill a short glass
50ml gin
50ml sugar syrup
  (see TIP on page 164)
150ml pink grapefruit juice
sprig of fresh rosemary,
  to garnish

MAKES 1 DRINK

Have you ever come across something that was the embodiment of someone you knew? No? Well I have. When I found out there was a cocktail called the Greyhound which was a mixture of gin and juice, I couldn't believe I hadn't heard of it. This. Was. Grace. In a short glass, poured over ice, it was the exact embodiment of my friend. A little sweet, a little sharp and a whole lotta delish — this is for my soul sister.

----

❶ Fill a short glass with crushed ice. Pour the gin over the ice, closely followed by the sugar syrup. Top up with the grapefruit juice.

❷ Bash the rosemary lightly in your hands, keeping it in its long, pine-tree shape. Use this to stir everything together nicely, and enjoy.

PEAR AND ROSEMARY TOM COLLINS

FOR THE TOM COLLINS
----

ice cubes,
  to fill a tall glass
50ml gin
30ml sugar syrup
  (see TIP on page 164)
10ml lemon juice
sprig of fresh rosemary,
  to garnish
10ml pear purée
160ml soda water

MAKES 1 DRINK

The origins of the Tom Collins cocktail are a little shrouded in mystery — or maybe a two-hundred-year-long hangover. Some people place it in Ireland, some in London, some in New York or Pennsylvania. Then some wild cards place it to St Louis. I like to think that somewhere there is a Mr Thomas Collins, sipping on gin and soda, grinning to himself like the drummer from Coldplay. World-famous and yet infinitely unrecognised.

----

❶ Fill a tall glass with ice cubes, then add the gin, sugar syrup and lemon juice. Bash the rosemary lightly between your hands to release its aromatic oils.

❷ Add the pear purée and use the rosemary sprig as a stirrer to mix everything together well.

❸ Top up with soda water and serve.

HURRICANE

FOR THE HURRICANE

ice cubes,
   to fill a tall glass
50ml white rum
25ml dark rum
50ml smooth orange juice
50ml passion fruit juice
50ml grenadine
25ml lime juice
1 maraschino cherry,
   to garnish

MAKES 1 DRINK

Hurricanes are the ultimate ugly duckling tale. They started out as a way to use up the last little bits of rum that no one wanted to drink neat. The rum usually found in an original hurricane was a bit rubbish and cheap, and so bartenders had to think of a way to get rid and still cut the cash. So they poured it into a hurricane glass, topped it up with juice, grenadine and a maraschino cherry, and made a killing.

❶ Fill a large, tall glass with ice cubes. Pour the rums, orange juice, passion fruit juice, grenadine and lime juice into a large jam jar and shake well.

❷ Pour the liquor into the ice-filled glass and top with the maraschino cherry. Serve with an ample amount of jazz playing in the background.

MINT JULEP

FOR THE MINT JULEP

5g fresh mint leaves (reserve
   a sprig for the garnish)
crushed ice, to shake, plus
   more to fill a short glass
50ml bourbon
   (I like Buffalo Trace
   or Maker's Mark the best)
icing sugar, to dust

MAKES 1 DRINK

Although a mint julep is technically a cocktail, this is not one for those who think a piña colada is a hard drink. It is essentially straight bourbon tempered with a touch of ice and a hint of mint. A drink for Southerners and strong stomachs.

❶ Put the mint leaves in the bottom of a short glass (a whiskey tumbler is ideal) and muddle them by pounding gently with the end of a rolling pin.

❷ Fill a jam jar with crushed ice and add the bourbon. Shake together for 1 minute. Fill the minty tumbler with more crushed ice and strain the liquor through a small sieve into the glass.

❸ Using a spoon, give everything a quick mix in the glass, then garnish with your reserved prettiest sprig of mint and a dusting of icing sugar.

> **TIP:** To make 500ml Basic sugar syrup, put 500ml cold water and 200g granulated sugar in a small saucepan over a gentle heat and dissolve the sugar, stirring occasionally. Bring the syrup to the boil for 1 minute. Remove from the heat, leave to cool and use in all the cocktails you can dream of.

SHIRLEY TEMPLE AT 21

FOR THE SHIRLEY TEMPLE

ice cubes,
   to fill a tall glass
50ml vodka
180ml ginger ale
10ml grenadine
4 maraschino cherries,
   to garnish

MAKES 1 DRINK

If you are going to have a virgin cocktail, there is nothing more innocent, more sickly-sweet and more joyful than a Shirley Temple. Named after the cotton-candy-haired child star, this is super-easy to make and perfect for a party. Having said that, why not make it a *real* party and, well, spike it. I've added a healthy dash of vodka here to make sure this drink stays away from the kids' table and firmly at the bar.

❶ Fill a tall glass with ice cubes. Pour over the vodka and then the ginger ale.

❷ Add the grenadine, but don't stir it in fully. It looks way nicer if it's left to trickle down carelessly.

❸ Top with the cherries and feel about as badass as that kid who spikes the punch at prom.

BEETROOT BLOODY MARIA

FOR THE BLOODY MARIA

450g raw beetroot (about 3
   medium-sized beetroots)
665ml tomato juice
juice of 2 limes
175ml tequila
1¼ teaspoons grated horseradish
few drops of Worcestershire
   sauce, to taste
few drops of Tabasco sauce,
   to taste
pinch of freshly ground
   black pepper
ice cubes,
   to fill 4 glasses
2 red chillies, to garnish
celery sticks, to garnish
a small bunch of fresh mint
   sprigs, to garnish (optional)

MAKES 4 DRINKS

The thing that makes this a 'Maria' and not a 'Mary' is the tequila. The beets also turn it into a vivacious magenta. This cocktail is for my friend Mimi (or Maria as she is known by grown-ups and colleagues). A little spicy, a little earthy and a little boozy — just how I like my friends.

❶ Preheat the oven to 180°C/gas mark 4. Cut the tops off the beets and wrap each one in foil. Place in a roasting tray and cook for 2 hours until really soft. You want to be able to break them apart with the handle of a teaspoon.

❷ Remove the beets from the oven and leave to cool fully before rubbing the peel off between gloved hands. Then break up into chunks and place in a blender along with the tomato and lime juices. Blitz until you have a smooth, thick, magenta mix. Add the tequila, horseradish, Worcestershire sauce, Tabasco and black pepper, and blitz again.

❸ Fill four large glasses with ice cubes and pour the Maria over the top. Slice the chillies in half lengthways and use along with the celery and mint to garnish.

HARD SHAKES

SERVES 2

I love any drink where the alcohol is masked just enough by ice cream and sprinkles. Can you honestly say that if it were a toss up between a boozy chocolate milkshake and a glass of something altogether grown-up you *wouldn't* pick the milkshake?!

I always think a shake is best served in a maximum of two portions. The idea of sharing a shake fills me with horror and dread, so if we each get our own there are no fights, no squabbles and no brain freezes as we each suck as hard as we can to finish the glass before the other.

FOR THE SHAKES

370g good-quality vanilla
   ice cream
85g smooth peanut butter
70ml Kirsch
160g cherry compote
whipped cream, to garnish
2 maraschino cherries,
   to garnish

PEANUT BUTTER AND JELLY

❶ Whizz the ice cream and peanut butter together in a blender until smooth. Don't do this for too long or the ice cream will melt too much.

❷ Add the Kirsch and cherry compote, and blitz again until you have a colour that can only be described as 'Pretty in Pink'.

❸ Pour into two milkshake glasses. Serve with a kiss of whipped cream and a cherry on top.

370g mint choc chip ice cream
70ml crème de menthe
whipped cream, to garnish
dark chocolate shavings,
   to garnish

MENTHE CHOC CHIP

❶ Scoop the ice cream into a blender and pour over the crème de menthe. Blitz until you have a vibrant green delight and then pour into two milkshake glasses.

❷ Garnish with a flourish of whipped cream and a sprinkling of chocolate shavings.

370g good-quality vanilla
   ice cream
80g Oreos
100ml Baileys
3 tablespoons Ovaltine powder,
   Milo or any chocolate
   malt powder

COOKIES AND IRISH CREAM

❶ Place the ice cream in a blender. Lightly break up the Oreos and add them to the blender, followed by the Baileys. Blitz until smooth, then add the Ovaltine powder and blitz again.

❷ Pour into two milkshake glasses and enjoy.

GROWN-UP FLOATS

MAKES 1 FLOAT

Anyone who's anyone who loves ice cream and soda will love an ice-cream float. Ice cream, plus soda pop, plus one long spoon and an even longer straw is the national symbol for happiness in the USA.

I always thought these should be a little more adult-friendly. Some things are great in childhood for a reason, but did a touch of rum here or there ever make desserts worse? Didn't think so. Fair warning though, these can sneak up on you, so line your stomach well beforehand. Preferably with my Double cheeseburger (page 57) and an imminent duvet day.

FOR THE FLOATS

215ml Coca-Cola
50ml spiced rum
70g ginger ice cream
  (about 2 balls)

215ml orange soda
50ml Cointreau
70g clotted cream ice cream
  (about 2 balls)

215ml root beer
50ml honey whiskey
  (or 50ml regular whiskey
  and 1 tablespoon clear
  honey whisked together)
70g vanilla ice cream
  (about 2 balls)

COKE AND SPICED RUM FLOAT

----

❶ Pour the Coca-Cola, closely followed by the rum, into a tall glass – a milkshake glass is best.

❷ Top with the ice cream and serve with a straw (for the liquor) and a long spoon (for the ice-cream treat).

ORANGES AND CREAM FLOAT

----

❶ Pour the orange soda and Cointreau into a tall glass.

❷ Top with the ice cream balls and serve immediately. Have a handy wipe close by – this is a sticky one.

ROOT BEER AND HONEY WHISKEY FLOAT

----

❶ Pour the root beer and honey whiskey (or whiskey and honey) into a tall glass.

❷ Top with the ice cream balls and devour right away.

SOUTHERN SWEET TEA

FOR THE SWEET TEA

200g caster sugar

7 English Breakfast teabags

1 lemon, sliced

ice cubes, to serve

SERVES 5

Americans, particularly Southerners, are obsessed with sweet tea in the same way Brits are obsessed with regular tea or Australians with flat whites. You can walk into any diner, café, bar or gas station across the South and find ice-cold pitchers of sugar-kissed amber nectar all over the show. And it is so wonderfully easy to make that you will never buy a bottle from the supermarket ever again.

----

❶ Put 2.5 litres of cold water and the sugar into a large saucepan and bring to the boil. Stir to dissolve all the sugar, then remove from the heat and add the teabags.

❷ Leave the tea to cool completely – about 2 hours – before removing the teabags.

❸ Add the lemon slices to the tea and ladle into a jug packed with ice cubes. Perfect to pretend you are on a porch somewhere a little south of the Mason–Dixon line.

MOONSHINE

FOR THE MOONSHINE
----

ice cubes, to shake, plus extra
  to fill a tall glass

50ml whiskey

130ml cranberry juice

70ml peach juice

a small handful of fresh
  mint leaves

60ml ginger beer

1 peach, stoned and cut into
  thin slices, to garnish

MAKES 1 DRINK

Moonshine itself is a kind of hoochy, vodka-y, corn whiskey combo where anything that could be made into alcohol is. It is a really general term for homemade spirit and in the sense of keeping all things casual and truly Southern, you can use any liquor you like here. I've kept it truly Tennessee with whiskey, but vodka or white rum would taste damn fine too.

----

❶ Put the ice cubes, whiskey and cranberry and peach juices in a jam jar and shake well.

❷ Put the mint leaves in a tall glass and muddle with the end of a rolling pin to release their gorgeous oils. Tip more ice cubes into the minty glass.

❸ Strain the shaken moonshine through a small sieve over the ice and mint. Top up with ginger beer and use a long spoon to mix together. Slip some peach slices down the side of the glass and enjoy immediately.

INDEX

A
apples:
apple fritters with goat's cheese 39
Yiddish French toast with caramelised apples 37
avocados:
foolproof guacamole 131

B
bacon:
old-fashioned waffles with maple bacon 20
peanut butter and bacon burgers 53
bagels with home-cured lox and schmear 19
Baileys:
cookies and Irish cream hard shake 168
Baja fish tacos 121
bananas foster, never-fail pancakes with 23
BBQ spring onions with rosemary and hazelnut
butter 64
beans, Boston baked 83
beef:
beer and juniper-braised beef brisket 49
classic beef pot roast 72
peanut butter and bacon burgers 53
real Texan chilli 50
steak tacos 117
beer and juniper-braised beef brisket 49
beetroot Bloody Maria 167
beignets, New Orleans 110
biscuits:
biscuits and sausage gravy 107
Key lime pie 139
s'mores cheesecake 140
black beans, enchiladas with roasted squash and 122
Bloody Maria, beetroot 167
blueberries:
blueberry and cinnamon pancakes 24
grilled buffalo steak with pickled blueberry
sauce 48
white chocolate, cranberry and blueberry
scones 34
Boston baked beans 83
Boston cream pie 145
bourbon:
mint julep 164
bread:
fry bread with fixin's 87
quick and easy cornbread 33
Yiddish French toast 37
brioche:
lobster rolls 81
broccoli:
grilled broccoli with oregano and crispy garlic 65
buffalo steak, grilled 48
burgers:
double cheeseburgers 57
peanut butter and bacon burgers 53
smoky pork burgers 56
butter:
butter-baked Cajun prawns 96
fiery green butter 61
orange and maple butter 61
rosemary and hazelnut butter 64
buttermilk 10
buttermilk fried chicken 93

C
cabbage:
ruby-red slaw 62
sweetheart, courgette and basil slaw 62
Cajun prawns, butter-baked 96
Cajun snapper, blackened 102

cakes:
black cherry and chocolate cupcakes 157
pink grapefruit cake 156
red velvet birthday cake 152
salted caramel pretzel pound cake 149
caramel:
salted caramel pretzel pound cake 149
ceviche, radish 129
challah French toast 37
cheese:
apple fritters with goat's cheese 39
best ever mac 'n' cheese 84
Cheddar and caraway seed hushpuppies 103
chicken Parmesan 75
double cheeseburgers 57
fry bread with fixin's 87
plantain tacos with queso fresco 123
posole salad 130
queso ahumado 126
cheesecake, s'mores 140
cherries:
black cherry and chocolate cupcakes 157
peanut butter and jelly shakes 168
chicharrones 127
chicken:
buttermilk fried chicken 93
chicken Parmesan 75
cider can chicken 58
nola chicken and sausage gumbo 97
Southern fried chicken and waffles 77
chillies 11
beetroot Bloody Maria 167
chilli tomato relish 27
real Texan chilli 50
steak tacos with chilli and bitter chocolate 117
chocolate:
black cherry and chocolate cupcakes 157
Boston cream pie 145
chocolate, hazelnut and sea salt toaster tarts 32
chocolate peppermint whoopie pies 143
cranberry, blueberry and white chocolate
scones 34
menthe choc chip shake 168
red velvet birthday cake 152
s'mores cheesecake 140
steak tacos with chilli and bitter chocolate 117
chorizo:
chorizo and mint flautas 118
mussel and chorizo jambalaya 94
chowder, New England clam 82
cider can chicken 58
clams:
New England clam chowder 82
San Francisco spaghetti with clams 78
cobbler, peach, orange and honey 146
Coca-Cola: Coke and spiced rum float 171
Jack and Coke pulled pork 46
coconut prawn tostadas 129
cookies:
cookies and Irish cream hard shake 168
snickerdoodles 155
corn 13
blackened corn on the cob – all dressed up 61
cornmeal:
Marcellus' corn muffins 31
quick and easy cornbread 33
courgettes:
sweetheart, courgette and basil slaw 62
crab cake po' boy 104
cranberries:
Moonshine 172

white chocolate, cranberry and blueberry
scones 34
cream cheese:
bagels with home-cured lox and schmear 19
red velvet pancakes with cream cheese drizzle 22
s'mores cheesecake 140
crème de menthe:
menthe choc chip shake 168
cupcakes, black cherry and chocolate 157
curried peanut soup 106

D
dressing, herby 100
drinks 163–172

E
eggs:
latkes with chilli tomato relish and fried eggs 27
redneck eggs benedict 28
enchiladas with roasted squash, black beans
and marjoram 122

F
fiery green butter 61
fish 12
bagels with home-cured lox and schmear 19
Baja fish tacos 121
blackened Cajun snapper 102
fixin's, fry bread with 87
flautas, chorizo and mint 118
floats, grown-up 171
French toast, challah 37
fritters, apple 39

G
gin:
Grace's Greyhound 163
pear and rosemary Tom Collins 163
ginger ale:
Shirley Temple at 21 167
ginger beer:
Moonshine 172
Grace's Greyhound 163
granola, pistachio, honey and ginger 38
grapefruit:
Grace's Greyhound 163
pink grapefruit cake 156
gravy, biscuits and sausage 107
green goddess quesadillas 124
grits, shrimp & 99
grown-up floats 171
guacamole, foolproof 131
gumbo, nola chicken and sausage 97

H
ham, whiskey molasses-glazed baked 71
hard shakes 168
hazelnuts:
hazelnut chocolate toaster tarts 32
rosemary and hazelnut butter 64
s'mores cheesecake 140
herby dressing 100
hollandaise sauce 28
hominy:
posole salad 130
Hurricane 164
hushpuppies, Cheddar and caraway seed 103

I
ice cream:
grown-up floats 171

hard shakes 168

J
Jack and Coke pulled pork 46
jambalaya, mussel and chorizo 94
jelly:
    peanut butter and jelly shakes 168

K
Key lime pie 139

L
latkes with chilli tomato relish and fried eggs 27
lemon chess pie 150
limes:
    cayenne and lime soured cream 61
    Key lime pie 139
    lime soured cream 104
lobster rolls 81

M
Marcellus' corn muffins 31
marinara sauce, sweet 76
marshmallows:
    s'mores cheesecake 140
meat 10
    old-fashioned meatloaf 76
    see also beef; pork, etc
Memphis dry-rub baby back ribs 45
mint julep 164
Moonshine 172
muffins, Marcellus' corn 31
mussel and chorizo jambalaya 94

N
New England clam chowder 82
New Orleans beignets 110
nola chicken and sausage gumbo 97

O
okra:
    nola chicken and sausage gumbo 97
old-fashioned meatloaf 76
onions, pink pickled 123
orange soda:
    oranges and cream float 171
oranges:
    orange and maple butter 61
    peach, orange and honey cobbler 146
oysters, deep-fried 100

P
pancakes:
    blueberry and cinnamon pancakes 24
    never-fail pancakes with bananas foster 23
    red velvet pancakes with cream cheese drizzle 22
pasta:
    best ever mac 'n' cheese 84
    chicken Parmesan 75
    San Francisco spaghetti with clams 78
peach juice:
    Moonshine 172
peaches:
    dixie peach salsa 54
    peach, orange and honey cobbler 146
peanut butter:
    peanut butter and bacon burgers 53
    peanut butter and jelly shakes 168
peanuts:
    curried peanut soup 106
pear and rosemary Tom Collins 163
peas:

green goddess quesadillas 124
peppermint:
    chocolate peppermint whoopie pies 143
pico de gallo 121
pies:
    Boston cream pie 145
    Key lime pie 139
    lemon chess pie 150
    pumpkin pie 144
    spiced sweet potato pie 109
pig skin:
    chicharrones 127
pistachio, honey and ginger granola 38
plantain tacos 123
po' boy, crab cake 104
pork:
    Jack and Coke pulled pork 46
    Memphis dry-rub baby back ribs 45
    old-fashioned meatloaf 76
    smoky pork burgers 56
posole salad 130
potatoes:
    latkes 27
praline crunch, walnut 31
prawns:
    butter-baked Cajun prawns 96
    coconut prawn tostadas 129
    shrimp and grits 99
pretzels:
    salted caramel pretzel pound cake 149
pumpkin pie 144

Q
quesadillas, green goddess 124
queso ahumado 126

R
radish ceviche 129
red velvet birthday cake 152
red velvet pancakes 22
redneck eggs benedict 28
relish, chilli tomato 27
rice 13
    mussel and chorizo jambalaya 94
ruby-red slaw 62
rum:
    Coke and spiced rum float 171
    Hurricane 164

S
salads:
    posole salad 130
    slaws 62
salmon:
    bagels with home-cured lox and schmear 19
salsa:
    dixie peach salsa 54
    green tomatillo salsa 132
    pico de gallo 121
    salsa roja 132
salted caramel pretzel pound cake 149
San Francisco spaghetti with clams 78
sandwiches:
    crab cake po' boy 104
sausages:
    biscuits and sausage gravy 107
    chorizo and mint flautas 118
    home-smoked hot links 54
    nola chicken and sausage gumbo 97
scones, white chocolate, cranberry and blueberry 34
Shirley Temple at 21 167

shortcakes, strawberry and basil 151
shrimp and grits 99
slaws 62
smoking food 12
s'mores cheesecake 140
snapper, blackened Cajun 102
snickerdoodles 155
soup:
    curried peanut soup 106
    New England clam chowder 82
soured cream:
    cayenne and lime soured cream 61
    lime soured cream 104
southern sweet tea 172
spring onions, BBQ 64
squash, enchiladas with roasted 122
strawberry and basil shortcakes 151
sweet potato pie, spiced 109
syrup 11

T
tacos:
    Baja fish tacos 121
    plantain tacos 123
    steak tacos 117
tea, southern sweet 172
tequila:
    beetroot Bloody Maria 167
Texan chilli, real 50
toaster tarts, hazelnut chocolate 32
Tom Collins, pear and rosemary 163
tomatillo salsa, green 132
tomatoes:
    beetroot Bloody Maria 167
    chilli tomato relish 27
    foolproof guacamole 131
    fry bread with fixin's 87
    salsa roja 132
    sweet marinara sauce 76
tortillas:
    chorizo and mint flautas 118
    coconut prawn tostadas 129
    enchiladas 122
    green goddess quesadillas 124
tostadas, coconut prawn 129

V
veal:
    old-fashioned meatloaf 76
vodka:
    Shirley Temple at 21 167

W
waffles:
    old-fashioned waffles with maple bacon 20
    Southern fried chicken and waffles 77
walnuts:
    challah French toast with caramelised apples
        and walnuts 37
    walnut praline crunch 31
whiskey:
    Moonshine 172
    root beer and honey whiskey float 171
    whiskey molasses-glazed baked ham 71
whoopie pies, chocolate peppermint 143

ACKNOWLEDGEMENTS

There are so many people that I want to thank it's almost impossible to know where to begin.

Although, I think first and foremost I have to thank my agent Martine Carter and Mimi Kroll at Sauce Management for taking a chance on me. When I came to Sauce I was unknown, untrained and unqualified and their faith in me has been both overwhelmingly flattering and equally mad! They are goddesses. Thank you.

It also goes without saying that this book would still be a fantasy of mine without Kyle Cathie of Kyle Books and Vicky Orchard, my editor. By putting my words into print you have made me the happiest kid in class – this book has been a dream of mine to write for so many years so thank you for making it come true.

This book was written alongside starting a brand new job at Ginger Jar Food and I want to make sure my colleagues know just how great they have been in teaching me more about food and cheffing than I ever thought I could know and being so encouraging the whole way along. Ross, Clare, Jenny – you're the best!

If it wasn't for Leiths School of Food and Wine I would still be crystallising caramel sauces and cooking porridge in a microwave. Well, I still do that to be fair, but I would be pretty clueless without the phenomenal training they gave me. And especially thank you to my class teacher Heli Miles who put up with my tears and terrible jokes for a solid 9 months. What a lady!

I would also like to thank my school History teacher Paula Hailstone, here. I have a love of learning about the past that could only be rivalled by my love of cooking and I don't know if I would have realised that without her. American food is like eating your way through History because every recipe has such a place in the timeline of that country, as I hope I've shown in this book. To know American food is to know its past and to connect with the people who lived it. She taught me to always ask more questions, always learn more, always do your research. She also put up with me for 7 years so, again, what a lady!

I've travelled the States countless times but by far the best trip I took was with my best friend, Grace Higgins. My other half, my number one soul sister, my person who makes the much wiser decisions for me – there is no WAY I would have as much fun, or make as many pop culture references, or drink as many chai lattes without you. Thank you for hanging out with me, eating with me, and travelling with me. As Charlotte said to Wilbur, you have been my friend and that in itself is a marvellous thing.

I would like to thank all of my friends, and Warren, who have been so supportive and excited as I have been about this project, including my friends in the States – I see you!

Lastly, this book is for my family. I wouldn't have lived in the States without them, I wouldn't have explored the whole country without them and I wouldn't have fallen in love with the food without them. Thank you to my brother, Edward, for his incredible creative talent and sharp wit. To my mum, Caroline for her insatiable curiosity and brilliant mind. To my dad, John, for his unending wanderlust and love of exploration.

And most importantly, thank you to the people of America, who have taken me in, fed me dinner and let me be a part of your awesome club. What a beautiful and awe-inspiring place. Thank you for letting me be a part of it.